Applying Artificial Intelligence to Project Management

Applying Artificial Intelligence to Project Management

Paul Boudreau

© 2019 by Paul Boudreau
All rights reserved. This book or any portion thereof may not be reproduced or used in any manner whatsoever without the express written permission of the publisher except for the use of brief quotations in a book review.
ISBN: 9781687550941

For my students

Contents

Prologue ix
Introduction xi

Chapter 1 AI for Project Management 1
    Is Anyone Concerned? 2
    Why Project Management? 5
    Machine Learning 8
    Providing Value: The Business Case 16
    Don't Be Misled 19
    The Problem with Automating Project Management Tasks 20
    Summary 24

Chapter 2 The Importance of Data 27
    Garbage In 28
    Data Volume 31
    Data Dependency 32
    Accessing the Data 37
    Data Mining 38
    How to Prepare the Data 40
    Summary 48

Chapter 3 Sample AI Tools 51
    Predicting Project Success 52
    AI for Stakeholder Management 65
    Virtual Assistants 83
    Resolving Issues Successfully 94
    An AI Change Control Tool 98
    Additional AI Tools and Resources 103
    Summary 107

Chapter 4	The Project Methodology	109
	Project Initiation	110
	Project Planning	111
	Project Execution	113
	Project Control	116
	Project Close	119
	Project Termination	120
	Agile Implementation	120
	Can AI Fix Project Failure?	122
	Summary	127
Chapter 5	Acquiring AI Tools	129
	Evaluating and Acquiring AI Tools	130
	Strategy for Implementing AI Tools	132
	How to Implement AI Tools	135
	A Roadmap	138
	Summary	142
Chapter 6	The Future of AI Tools for Project Management	143
	The Project Manager and the Project Team	144
	Is AI Intelligent?	148
	AI and Ethics	152
	The Rapid Advance of AI Tools	154
	Summary	155
Chapter 7	Conclusion	157

References	161
Lectures and Talks	167
Acknowledgments	169
About the Author	171

Prologue

A number of years ago, after I finished teaching the last class of a project management course, one of my students asked me why I had not written a book. He said that I had many personal stories that would be interesting for people to read. Writing a book is more difficult than people imagine, and personal anecdotes are often interesting in the context of a classroom, especially when they relate to course material. However, this does not necessarily translate well into a written work. It was only during my research into artificial intelligence (AI) for project management that I remembered the challenge.

Although I have a long employment history in the information technology industry, I don't consider myself an expert in AI technology. My expertise is in the merging of the possibilities of AI tools and the process of project management. My overriding objective for the concepts presented here is to improve project success rates. I have been a project manager on both highly successful projects and a number of not so successful projects. I much prefer the successful ones. My AI experience initially involved learning some R and Python programming, and later I wrote the initial Python code for a simple but effective machine learning predictor tool. With this book, I hope to bridge the gap between the technology and the project management processes.

It is my students who inspire me. They sit through my lectures then surprisingly show up as volunteers at local Project Management Institute (PMI) conferences or talks that I give on project management. They have both energy and passion, and I hope that I can inspire them as much as they inspire me.

Introduction

Projects are notoriously late, over budget, and very difficult to control. It's time to focus on how to really achieve project success. Hopefully, this book will help readers understand how AI tools will change project management. The rationale for using AI in projects is important and is, therefore, where the book begins. This is followed by an overview of how to find the value in using AI tools.

Chapter 2 is about data, the critical element in this technology. Of course, data is important for all software but even more so for machine learning algorithms. This section discusses the data required to provide input to a machine learning algorithm. It includes data availability, format, and the difficulties that will be encountered with data. Guidance is also provided for how to prepare and manage the data needed to feed AI tools.

The exciting part is chapter 3, which contains a description of sample tools that are in progress or already available for project management. While the concepts behind these are both fascinating and very practical, they are not without problems. This section is a review of existing and potential tools that can be used to change the way that projects are managed. AI is a technology being deployed into all aspects of our lives, and more projects will have an objective of implementing AI into numerous organizations. Imagine trying to implement AI without actually having any AI in the project methodology! It's like trying to write the entire contents of Wikipedia using a typewriter. Eventually you will get it done, but it will take a long time, and correcting errors is a gruesome process.

A review of a generic project methodology is in chapter 4, and it is intended to stimulate thoughts about how AI can fit into the project processes for an organization. Since this is meant to be a practical guide, some suggestions are included on where to incorporate AI tools. This requires an understanding of both the potential value as well as the possibility of negative results.

Chapter 5 is about strategies to acquire and implement AI tools successfully. A structured approach will be needed to make process change successful. Vendors will be anxious to showcase tools that may or may not be effective for improving the project processes in your organization. There will be a tradeoff between taking a cautious approach to acquiring AI tools and the desire to improve project success rates as soon as possible.

The final chapter discusses what can be expected in the near future as AI tools advance in all areas of our everyday lives, and especially in project management. There will be changes to the activities performed by the project manager and the project team. Stakeholders will praise the new technology or disparage it as ineffective and wasteful. In addition to resolving issues such as security and privacy, project managers need to take advantage of the value that AI tools offer. That advantage is a dramatic improvement in project success rates.

CHAPTER 1
AI for Project Management

What if I gave you a tool that could increase your project success rate to 95 percent or more?

IS ANYONE CONCERNED?

The biggest challenge for project managers is to deliver the project scope on time and on or under budget. However, based on these easily calculated metrics, most projects are unsuccessful. Is anyone concerned? Not only are the current failure rates astounding, but they are also incredibly wasteful and should not be tolerated. As professional project managers, we are inundated by the litany of detailed reasons why projects fail. This is accompanied by a variety of entities that offer project manager training in order to "fix us." It's not working! The reason that it's not working is people are not the problem. Project managers and their teams work incredibly hard on project tasks in order to achieve a successful outcome only to face disappointment. Projects fail due to poor processes. We need to change *how* we perform project management. In fact, project methodologies need to be radically changed, and the answer is to use new technology. Artificial intelligence (AI), specifically machine learning tools, is the only way to increase project success rates to a significantly higher level than they are at today. AI tools need to disrupt the current project management processes so that we can all finally be proud of project success rates.

A pivotal moment that caught people's attention was when an IBM computer easily beat the reigning Jeopardy! television game show champion. Not only did the AI-based computer find the correct answers, but it also had perfect timing in order to be selected first to give the answer. AI has many capabilities, such as diagnosing an illness based on an x-ray image or MRI scan and using voice analysis to detect medical conditions such as post-traumatic stress disorder. The self-driving car is another example of AI technology, and it can be compared to project management. It has a clear objective to arrive at a destination and makes decisions as the car is moving. Along the way, it encounters a number of issues, and they are managed in order to achieve the goal. A project has numerous documents that contain the plan, which is essentially the strategy on how to achieve the outcome. As the project is executed, it encounters numerous obstacles, and the right decisions must be made. AI tools will enable the project to drive more easily and reach the destination on time and on budget.

Adding AI tools to the project management methodology will change the way projects are managed. At the start of the project, an AI tool will search all project documents and look for incomplete or misleading data. This is similar to how machine learning tools currently look at an x-ray image or MRI scan and make a diagnosis. What is the diagnosis for the project based on the image created with the current project documents? AI will also verify whether the implementation strategy will be successful. Based on the project documents, a prediction of project success will be made before the project starts and then as the project is executed, an AI tool will help guide and direct the project manager to make the best decisions in all situations. The trend of ongoing predictions throughout the project will highlight the ability of the project to stay on course, something that will be of high interest to the project's client or sponsor. The project execution stage will be guided by tools that optimize resources and constantly reevaluate risks. Managing communication will no longer be difficult, because it will be based on psychological profiles of stakeholders, and an AI tool will determine the best way to send clear and direct messages that will motivate and inspire project stakeholders. Project issues will be eliminated or minimized because they will be included in a risk plan or mitigated as part of the project strategy before the project starts. The project manager will be able to manage the project using a smartphone app with assistance and guidance from a well-trained virtual personal assistant that understands project management logic and how to make all the right decisions that will result in a successful project outcome. These are only some of the possibilities for applying AI to project management.

Artificial intelligence can be a confusing term, as it encompasses many fascinating aspects about how we use computer technology. The most appropriate meaning is the ability of machines to demonstrate some cognitive function similar to humans, such as decision-making. The devices and algorithms being created have enabled a multitude of new capabilities based on this technology. For this book, the focus is on machine learning, which is, in simple terms, the ability of a programmed algorithm to be trained to recognize and correlate patterns in data. The plan is to use these trained algorithms to improve the success rate of projects.

Machine learning is also an unusual term. The "machine" part simply refers to the system, such as a computer server or computer hardware, where the software is stored and the program is executed. The "learning" part is the algorithm that is trained based on input data in order to create a model that can be used to predict or classify a new set of data. It is the algorithm that does the learning, and the machine or hardware is where everything is computed and stored.

Another basic capability of AI is natural language processing (NLP). NLP is a computer program's ability to understand human language and classify communication into a meaning or, as it is called in NLP, an intent. It includes the ability to interpret emotion behind the words, which becomes part of a skill known as sentiment analysis. This is a very interesting characteristic because we all use words differently and have different backgrounds. NLP is also used to search documents and extrapolate meaning as well as determine correlations and anomalies. These algorithms can have a dramatic influence on how humans interact with machines now that machines can analyze and identify our behavior and uncover our personalities. NLP-based algorithms can be integrated into project management tools.

AI is a disruptive technology, and as project managers, we need to embrace that concept. It is similar to other new technologies in that it requires us to understand how to evaluate it, learn its value, and implement it properly. It is different in that it is a far more complex technology subject to wide misunderstanding and even fear. On the other hand, it has the potential to solve more problems and provide incredible value in many areas of our society, including in the field of project management. The biggest challenge at this early stage of using AI for project management is that we need to find creative ways to uncover the value so that adoption becomes more compelling.

AI will change our project processes, and it will certainly change the way we think about and manage projects. A lot of people claim this will "automate" tasks. Perhaps that is true, but not in the sense that you think of it. As the new AI tools are developed, it will become obvious that we cannot continue to manage projects the same old way, and this is a good thing. Imagine the benefits of much higher project success rates: fewer wasted resources, lower environmental impact, lower stress levels for the project team, and generally more positive results and positive energy. Above all, the value of consistently completing projects on time and on or under budget is enormous, and it will add a new credibility factor to project completion. Now, can we make it happen?

WHY PROJECT MANAGEMENT?

Project management is an interesting field. It is responsible for all the changes in the world, because it takes a project to make a change whether or not it is called a project. Projects are how new technology gets implemented, so it is only natural that project management itself should be the subject of new technology such as AI. A well-structured project will land people on Mars, and a project will find a cure for cancer. Yet we cannot continue to perform these incredible accomplishments with old tools. The time is right to inject AI into project management processes. This will not be easy. We struggle to understand new technologies, and due to the complexity of managing projects, there are no clear answers on how AI tools can be implemented successfully.

There are a variety of statistics on project failure rates, such as 68 percent of information technology (IT) projects fail, or 70 percent of organizations reported at least one project failure in the previous twelve months. In 2013 fewer than 33 percent of projects were successfully completed on time and on budget, and for every $1 billion invested in the United States, $122 million was wasted due to poor project performance.[1] Whatever the source of information, the success rate of projects is far less than 50 percent. For large projects it is probably closer to 30 percent, because numerous successful smaller projects can positively influence the average. Do we need machine learning tools in project management? It cannot happen quickly enough. There are an estimated 16.5 million project managers in the world, and these are the people who need to be encouraged to implement this new technology.[2]

Project results are the identifying markers of humanity. From the creation of pyramids to launching rockets into space, the list of completed projects is a tour of spectacular human achievements. A list of megaprojects in the world includes a vast array of initiatives. From aerospace to disaster cleanup to global sports events, the ability to complete a project demonstrates human progress.

---

1   The sources of failures rates are as follows:
Michael Krigsman, "Study: 68% of Projects Fail," ZDNet, January 14, 2009, https://www.zdnet.com/article/study-68-percent-of-it-projects-fail/
Alan Brame, Souella Cumming, Gina Barlow, Grant Avery, and Perry Woolley, "KPMG New Zealand Project Management Survey 2010," https://home.kpmg/nz/en/home/insights.html;, September, 2010,
Jim Crear et al, "The Standish Group Report: Chaos," https://www.projectsmart.co.uk/white-papers/chaos-report.pdf, accessed August 30, 2019.
Project Management Institute (PMI), "Pulse of the Profession Survey," https://www.pmi.org/about/press-media/press-releases/2018-pulse-of-the-profession-survey, February 15, 2018.
2   Dave Garrett, "How Many Projects Managers are in the US and Canada?," https://www.projectmanagement.com/blog-post/4226/How-many-Project-Managers-are-in-the-US-and-Canada-#targetText=Situation%3A%20You%20love%20obscure%20facts,Project%20Managers%20in%20the%20world., October 2011.

The purpose of a project is to create something new or achieve a result that has not been accomplished previously. Projects are the drivers of change in the world. Functional management consists of regularly repeated operations. It is far easier to implement machine learning tools in functional management because the same activities happen on a regular basis. Not only is every project unique, but the process used to implement projects varies greatly. The Project Management Institute (PMI) uses the Project Management Body of Knowledge (PMBOK) as a guide for project managers, but anyone who has worked on different projects realizes that although it would be nice to have a common process, it rarely happens. Project methodologies vary widely by project type or industry. They might have common issues such as risk and resource planning, but each project attempts to find a process or methodology that works for them, and it appears that a lot of projects have no predetermined process at all. That makes it more difficult to implement machine learning tools because it is more difficult to hit a moving target.

As projects adopt some of the AI tools used in a functional setting, such as organizing a meeting calendar, some efficiencies will be achieved. Maybe there is a new tool to automatically create a status report or identify the most efficient resources for a task. These are incremental gains, but what project management needs now are game-changing improvements. Project management needs tools that will increase the project success rate to 95 percent or higher on a consistent basis. That is the potential for AI in project management. Can we adopt the tools that will result in an incredible improvement in project results? I believe we can. However, AI is a new and complex technology. We need to be smart enough to understand the concepts and technical knowledge as well as creative enough to find ways to insert the right tools into the process.

For organizations that already have good success in projects, the formula is going to change. Projects are becoming more complex, and the environment is becoming more complicated. The world of work is becoming personalized, customized, and globalized. Success today does not guarantee success in the future, so continuation of a winning project implementation methodology means including changes that will have a positive impact on the outcome.

MACHINE LEARNING

The ultimate objective for machine learning is to use the data to do one of two things: *prediction* or *classification*. At its core, the algorithm uses a mathematical formula based in calculus that attempts to find the least error between correlations in the data. This is also known as minimizing the cost function. Machine learning is not an expert system or a simulator. I worked on simulation software for a number of years in the past. It is good at running multiple scenarios and allowing you to select the "best" one, or the one with the greatest probability of success. An AI or machine learning tool looks at the same data and develops a correlation that is not evident to a human brain. From that correlation, and assuming there is enough training data, the AI software makes a prediction. On the other hand, the Monte Carlo simulation is normally used to model the probability of different outcomes and only says, "Here are a number of possible outcomes," or, "Here is the most likely outcome." The advantage of AI is accuracy. The disadvantage is the need to have an appropriate amount of training data to make a valid prediction. The advantage of Monte Carlo is that it gives a range of possibilities to consider based on the available data. The disadvantage is that it is not really making a prediction but only illustrating the variety of possible successful outcomes. Both use statistical methods, but the AI algorithm tries to "learn" from the data.

A machine learning tool is built using software such as Python programming language and uses utilities to create decision-making algorithms, arguably the most effective one being a neural network.

Learning occurs in a number of ways, but the most common include the following.

Supervised learning is where a dataset is labeled and the algorithm is trained to correlate each dataset with the labeled result. The algorithm is capable of modifying itself until it has the most accurate model. It is then used on test data to verify the accuracy of the model. Supervised learning is used in the field of health to diagnose x-ray results and can provide higher accuracy than a trained technician.[3] The algorithm is trained on x-ray images labeled as either clear or showing evidence of a condition. A new x-ray image with a unique pattern is used as input to the algorithm, and it diagnoses or predicts the result.

For projects we can also label our datasets. There are successful projects, well-executed risk plans, and communication plans that result in high stakeholder satisfaction. There are also negative results for each example.

Unsupervised learning is where the data is not labeled, but with a sufficient number of clues, the algorithm will be able to classify the data effectively. If the data indicates that an object has leaves, a trunk, and branches, then the algorithm will correctly classify it as a tree. The main benefit of unsupervised learning is clustering. The algorithm has no labels and simply groups similar items together. This is frequently used in recommender systems where if you like a certain book or movie, the algorithm looks at similar books or movies and recommends that you purchase them. How can this be applied to projects? Perhaps certain types of projects or organizations are prone to specific risks. Risks can be clustered or grouped so that when one of the risks from a cluster occurs, there might be a strong possibility that a similar risk will occur. If one type of problem occurs in a specific organization, then it

---

3 Hanae Armitage, "X-ray Results Can Provide Higher Accuracy than a Trained Technician," Medical Xpress, November, 2018, https://medicalxpress.com/news/2018-11-ai-outperformed-radiologists-screening-x-rays.html.

may be likely that problems classified as similar will also occur. There are many other possibilities, and researchers and practitioners need to find the correlations in the data and create the appropriate algorithms to increase the success rates for their projects.

Reinforcement learning is when the algorithm learns through trial and error to make proper predictions. A common example is when you type on a smartphone and the full word appears after only two or three letters. The program learns your pattern through a series of repetitions where you did not select the word it suggested because that was not the word you wanted. This happened with my business name, "Stonemeadow," which is unusual and not in a dictionary. At first, I ignored the recommendation and typed in the word correctly. On the second try, it again recommended other endings, but by the third attempt, the smartphone learned that the most likely word is "Stonemeadow," and after typing the first few letters it correctly shows me the option of the word that I want.

How can this apply to project management? All algorithms need to be updated on a regular basis in order to stay accurate, and this is one of the methods for doing so. Also, it is ideally suited for agile projects containing numerous iterations that each have the opportunity to improve on the previous one to create a better result. Additional examples are provided later in the book.

Rules-based learning involves capturing a set of rules that represent the knowledge about the data. Instead of having a single model, this approach can be used in different situations in order to arrive at a prediction. Individual rules are not models, but the condition determines which set of rules collectively create the prediction model.

The work in AI began decades ago, and some concepts are still relevant today. In an article published in 1950, Alan Turing proposed the concept that a machine learning tool does not have to be a perfectly complete model as long as it can be taught how to learn.[4] This concept is essential for successful AI in all areas and cannot be forgotten when using AI tools for project management. While other software applications require version upgrades, machine learning tools require data upgrades. In other words, you cannot simply deploy a machine learning tool then ignore it. In the book *Weapons of Math Destruction*, Cathy O'Neil outlines the absolutely vital requirement for a feedback loop. In her judgment there needs to be an ongoing input of fresh data that supports the training process in order to maintain accurate results. Important to the maintenance of machine learning tools will be software and data updates to ensure that the tools continue to produce proper results. AI tools that are developed as a child need more attention.

In the book *Superintelligence*, Nick Bostrom identifies two streams of AI. One is narrow AI, which focuses on achieving a specific objective, and the other is strong AI, which is known as artificial general intelligence or whole brain emulation. An artificial general intelligence is what most people fear, based on what is portrayed in fiction where a computer becomes smarter than humans and takes over the world. Having an algorithm that performs all functions is conceptually possible but has numerous practical difficulties. As with humans, a big computer brain needs resources to continue to exist, and those resources are not free. The most likely scenario is that we never completely develop artificial general intelligence but make amazing discoveries along the way.

The field of project management faces a similar narrow and general issue for machine learning tools. Can a model be developed that can determine and accomplish project success for all projects, regardless of factors such as size, function, and purpose, or will it require several subsets of project AI tools to be developed? This book is about narrow

---

[4] Alan Turing, "Computer Machinery and Intelligence," Mind, Volume LIX, Issue 236, October, 1950, pages 433-460.

AI specifically targeted for project-management-based machine learning algorithms that can be implemented in the project management processes.

The content below is a highly simplified explanation of how machine learning works. Please check the reference section at the end of the book for some great resources that provide far more depth. Remember in school when you took calculus and were annoyed because you thought it was something you would never need again? It turns out that you were wrong. At the heart of machine learning software is a calculus equation. Machine learning is essentially a software program coded in a language such as R, Python, or even Java. By the way, it's not called Python because of the snake but was named after a British television comedy show called Monty Python, but that's just trivia.

Python is an easy-to-learn, free, open-source programming language. It is concise and powerful and has numerous standard libraries or scripts that contain prewritten code. Python is one of the preferred languages for developing machine learning algorithms because it is simple to learn, has great data handling capacity, and includes complex mathematic equations in the standard libraries.

One important feature about software code, if you have never written any, is that it can use loops in order to execute the same command over and over again. This means that you can perform a function repeatedly for a specified number of times or until you meet a specified condition. Here is a simple example of a "for" loop in Python:

```
for i in range (1, 20):
    print df.loc[i]
```

This loop repeats twenty times, printing each character in the range, then stops. With a machine learning algorithm, a loop is used until the function achieves a specified condition. Inside the loop is a calculus equation. Think of a curve in a graph like the one in figure 1.0.

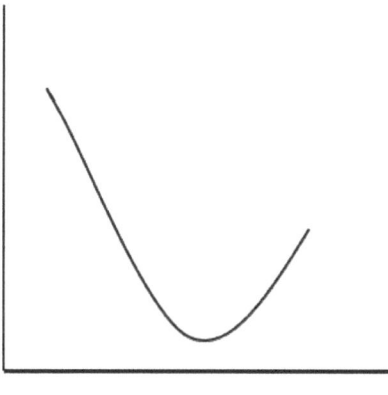

Figure 1.0

You start at the highest point on the left side of the curve, and you need to go down the curve mathematically until you find the lowest point. The machine learning algorithm to do this is called gradient descent. You are minimizing the error in a correlation between two variables. Another way to think of this is that you are optimizing the correlation between variables. In a neural network, there are many variables with many of these curves, and this technique is used to adjust the parameters of the model that is built. The learning part is the algorithm finding the optimum correlation, which is then used for classification or prediction. Fortunately, the algorithms for doing this can be accessed as functions from a library in Python, for example.

In order to work properly, a neural network uses forward propagation and back propagation to adjust the parameters known as weights and biases so that the result is the best fit for the model created. What are we trying to correlate? In a supervised learning model, the input data for the number of datasets is correlated to the label assigned to each dataset. A second loop is used that repeats the training process for a specified number of times, known as epochs, in order to make further adjustments to the weights and biases, which creates a more accurate model.

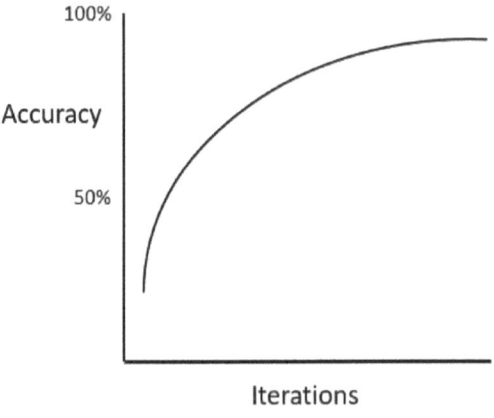

Figure 1.1

The graph in figure 1.1 shows how the algorithm *learns* to make the right correlations based on numerous iterations of adjusting weights and biases. If you want more details about this process, please check the definitions for the terms on reliable websites or look for appropriate books and introductory courses dedicated to the subject. This is not a complete explanation and is only an attempt to illustrate that the algorithm has a mathematical basis for calculating results.

Criticism of Artificial Intelligence
It can be difficult to accept new technologies, especially when they are coming at us with increasing speed. The comedian Orny Adams has a great routine about technology where he says that he already talks to too many things: his phone, his car, and his TV. He doesn't need a

talking fridge. "I've started to talk to stuff that doesn't even talk. I was yelling at the ceiling fan last week, going, 'Slow down!' [pause] 'Slow down! What are you? Dumb? Don't make me get off this couch and pull the cord!'" [5]

The massive array of AI technologies will frustrate and confuse us. As project managers we need to sort through the fog and provide leadership. That means we need to educate ourselves to understand the tools, ensure we select tools that provide value to the way we manage projects, find a way to make sure that stakeholders accept the new AI enabled processes, and implement the tools successfully. That's a big challenge.

There is reason to be cautious with AI tools, and once more a good source of concern is found in the book *Weapons of Math Destruction*. In the book, O'Neil discusses the importance of a feedback loop for machine learning algorithms and designers finding a way to best incorporate it. Historical data holds the danger that it is stuck in the past, and as humanity advances and adopts concepts such as universal human rights, a machine learning tool has a natural tendency to give current standards lower value in consideration of the vast amount of historical data. This is known as a hidden bias. We may believe in gender equality, but historical data will say otherwise, and a machine learning tool will be trained to recommend a male CEO for a corporation because that has been the standard in the past. Historical data promotes stereotypes and assumes that people are not capable of changing their behavior or beliefs, something that we know is not true. Project managers need to be aware of this and view it as a serious issue. How does the algorithm account for hidden bias in historical data? A serious issue deserves a serious response.

---

5   Orny Adams, "Who Needs a 'Smart' Fridge?" Just for Laughs Comedy Festival, Montreal, July 2019. Thanks to Team Orny Adams for permission. For more laughs check out his website, https://www.ornyadams.com/.

Another danger for AI tools is when they are created to provide a function and then abandoned. Think of an elevator installed in a new building. It works perfectly at first, but over time with the lack of proper maintenance or repair, it becomes less useful and possibly even fatal to the people it is trying to help. The same is true for machine learning algorithms. They need maintenance in the form of updates as well as the ability to grow and develop based on new data. Designers of programs must find an effective way to include reinforcement learning. Not only does this provide a mechanism for updating the machine learning outcome, but it also reduces, in some measure, the bias from historical data.

PROVIDING VALUE: THE BUSINESS CASE

There are numerous examples outside of project management that demonstrate successful implementation of AI tools and how the business or organization received a significant benefit.

In a survey by Deloitte, 11 percent of organizations reported a return of investment from AI of over 40 percent, and another 12 percent reported returns of 30 percent or more.[6] The value is normally expressed in terms of increased revenue or bottom-line cost savings. The value of deploying AI tools for project management also needs to be captured in a business case. The easiest way to express value is to identify the value of increasing the project success rates in the organization. In order to capture the financial impact, a review can be held of past projects that failed to meet the schedule or budget. The delays and budget overspending can be quantified and used to justify the cost of acquiring AI tools. Some projects incur penalties for missing

---

6 Jeff Loucks et al., "Future in the Balance? How Countries Are Pursuing an AI Advantage," Deloitte, May 1, 2019, https://www2.deloitte.com/insights/us/en/focus/cognitive-technologies/ai-investment-by-country.html.

schedule deadlines. Additional benefits can be found by quantifying the reduction in waste as well as resources that could have been reassigned to more productive activities or better utilized. It is more difficult to value the improved motivation of project team members who have greater confidence in project success. There may also be some positive environmental aspects to projects that have a higher success rate. Finally, there is great value in having an organization that consistently achieves goals such as meeting scheduled deadlines and preparing accurate project budgets. The client or sponsor of projects will favor project organizations and project teams that know how to win. Calculating the value of a business benefit is always easier to determine than the value of a human benefit, such as reducing stress or improving communications.

The process of acquiring AI tools to improve project methodology needs to include an analysis of costs compared to the value received by completing the project. The business case for implementing AI tools looks straightforward, but it has some significant challenges. In general, any tool that improves the project schedule or reduces project cost will provide value to an organization. Calculating the costs for implementation will require more intense review. Most organizations will face two serious implementation issues that need to be considered when calculating the deployment cost: data and single focus.

1. Data

> Experience in AI deployment projects shows that 60 to 80 percent of the effort will be spent finding and cleaning data.[7] Therefore, the business case needs to

---

7   Gil Press, "Cleaning Big Data: Most Time-Consuming, Least Enjoyable Data Science Task, Survey Says," *Forbes*, March 23, 2016, https://www.forbes.com/sites/gilpress/2016/03/23/data-preparation-most-time-consuming-least-enjoyable-data-science-task-survey-says/#11ec00896f63.

include the cost of data cleansing. Typical data issues include a one-time cost to clean existing data and then an ongoing cost to maintain clean data. It is possible that an organization will require a data architect to help define data standards and ongoing strategies to properly maintain the project data.

2. Single focus

   Implementing an AI tool to perform a single activity in project management is problematic because projects are integrated across several knowledge areas. An AI tool that finds a way to reduce the schedule by two weeks also needs to consider the side effects on risk, quality, and other areas across the project. Many AI tools in project management will have a simple, single purpose, so any unforeseen negative results and remediation must be considered for the business case.

While a single-focus AI tool may cause project issues, there are reasons to consider them. Think of the effort it takes for several people to evaluate a large request for proposal (RFP) document to decide whether to bid on the work. A trained machine learning tool will be able to use NLP to review the document and recommend what an acceptable bid would be. That in turn allows an appropriate decision to be made. Any activity that requires a lot of resources to be consumed through reading and analyzing documents on a project can be completed faster and more accurately using AI tools. A single-focus AI tool can also review a scope statement for completeness or inaccuracies. Capturing errors early in documents can be valuable since finding errors due to misleading or inaccurate documents is more costly as the project progresses.

Although the cost of an AI tool is added to a business case, it should be noted that one machine learning engine can be used for many solutions, which means that the price of using these tools should be reasonable and will cost less over time. A pay-per-use or subscriber-based cost model is common in technology today, and this model can be expected to continue with AI tools, assuming that a web-based cloud solution is acceptable to the organization. If not, then an on-premise solution is likely to be more costly, although it may be necessary due to the organization policies and procedures.

For project managers, creating a good business case is a significant achievement. It "sells" the project, motivates the team, and provides a clear objective. A well-constructed business case normally considers all costs, and for an AI deployment, some of those costs are less obvious.

Table 1: Sample of Business Case Considerations

Benefit	Costs
On time completion	Data preparation
On budget	Software cost
Reduced waste	Training
Resource allocation efficiency	Ongoing support and maintenance of the model
Environmental benefits	
Customer/client satisfaction	
Reduced impact on interdependent projects	

DON'T BE MISLED

It is easy to be fascinated by new and mysterious technology instead of thinking about how to create and deploy the technology for practical solutions. Machine learning is an algorithm created in software that is used by creative minds to do amazing things. The name "artificial intelligence" can evoke images of intrigue and sometimes even fear. AI is a specific field of technology that uses a number of different concepts to analyze data in order to make predictions and perform classification. A self-driving car is an example of AI because the machine learning logic makes decisions based on a variety of streaming information. An appliance like a dishwasher is not AI. Somewhere between a dishwasher and a self-driving car, people get confused about what is and is not AI. A robotic arm on an assembly line is not AI because it does the same task over and over again. In fact, the logic is preprogrammed and does not change unless there is manual intervention to adjust the programming code. Software programs that read x-ray images and determine a diagnosis more accurately than a technician are AI because the machine learning code has been trained to recognize and classify patterns that a human brain cannot. Perhaps the distinction is not clear because people believe that any device that replaces the capability of a human should be considered AI. The narrow view is that there are many electronic and programmed devices, but AI is different. It has a cognitive capability that is unique to how it operates.

I was helping to clean a house and found an old vacuum cleaner probably from the 1980s. It had a feature called a "smart" cord. The cord is pulled out to the desired length, and it stays that way while you vacuum. When the work is finished and it is time to reel in the cord, you press a button. This activates the spring inside the cord caddy, and the cord automatically reels itself back in. That's very clever. But is it "smart"? Does it have intelligence? We like to ascribe attention-grabbing words to products and ideas, so we have to be careful what those words actually mean. I don't think that vacuum cleaner was the beginning of artificial intelligence in home appliances.

THE PROBLEM WITH AUTOMATING PROJECT MANAGEMENT TASKS

The pace of technology development makes AI more practical every day. From self-driving vehicles to computers that beat humans at games, this technology can now access and process more information and do it faster than a human brain. As project managers we need to think about what changes have to take place in our project management processes and project documents in order to take advantage of the value that AI offers.

Project management remains a largely manually intensive function. The project manager creates a project management plan, which includes the project schedule, risk register, stakeholder register, and numerous other documents. The project manager also reviews changes, manages a project team, and communicates to stakeholders, which are all time-consuming activities. Currently the main automated tool in a project is the scheduling software, and this can only be considered truly automated if the project start date is created and the remaining activities are coded as dependencies.

There are a lot of tedious and repetitive project management tasks. For many activities, such as estimating, the majority of the work is done for one project and then is done again for a new project. Can these tasks be automated? Of course they can, but a more complex question is whether they need AI tools to do so. It is possible that expert systems can automate routine tasks, although using AI techniques may improve the accuracy? Some of the automated tools being implemented for functional and office managers will simply spill into the field of project management, and that will be an opportunity to take advantage of them.

Attempts have been made to automate some tasks such as creating status reports or capturing and communicating meeting notes, but these do not provide significant value to the project. Perhaps automation in project management is slow to materialize because each project is unique, and every project has a myriad of challenges and changes that are difficult to predict. Project management offices (PMOs) offer templates and hope that each project manager achieves a successful result. Integration of project management tools with the sponsoring organization's other existing software applications is a potential to help provide value but is also problematic. For example, there are time-tracking tools that can automatically update the project schedule by updating the time spent on an activity, and then the project manager can use the result to compare this to the forecast. However, estimating the original amount of time required on an activity then matching it to time spent is an imperfect equation. For example, assume an estimated activity is planned to consume forty hours with a variable of plus or minus 10 percent. Meanwhile the person working on the activity submits thirty hours, which may include some non-work-related time. If there is no indication of the task being completed, how do we know whether the activity is complete? Based on the time submitted, is the activity ahead or behind schedule? The problem with automation in the examples above is that there is no "intelligence" behind it, and this is exactly where AI contributes. It is AI development in project management that will drive automation, and without AI, the automation of activities will be protracted as well as be ineffective at achieving the dramatic increase in project success rates that is required. For AI it will be important to focus on the project management process or methodology. Once the project plans are created, how will automation be used to increase efficiency or improve the project success rate? Automation is a process that is repeated over and over again and is based on a fixed program. AI is the ability to learn from the data and make decisions in existing or new situations. The lure of automation for project management activities can confuse organizations into doing the wrong thing.

Vendors of existing project management tools can distract us from making the major changes that are needed. They are taking pieces of AI like predictive analytics and adding it to their tools. Here is an example. You have a schedule delay and are three days past your end date. The predictive analytics tool goes to work and recommends that Mary be replaced by George on her tasks and Ramesh be replaced by Khalid. These changes will bring the project back on track and recover the three days. Isn't AI wonderful? Not so fast. What about risk? What about quality? As project managers we need to consider all aspects of the project, and yet this approach is taking a piecemeal solution. If you follow PMI and PMBOK, there are ten knowledge areas: integration, scope, time, cost, resources, communication, quality, risk, procurement, and stakeholder management. It is important to take a holistic approach to the project, which means that all interactions between these knowledge areas must be considered. Similarly, it is important that AI tools take a holistic view of the project and not optimize one specific activity or area while ignoring or degrading an interconnected project activity.

    A positive example of using new technology can be explained with the implementation of large enterprise resources planning (ERP) or customer relationship management (CRM) software applications such as SAP, PeopleSoft, or Microsoft Dynamics. As part of the initial work, some organizations went around and looked at an employee's tasks. They listed the tasks and determined that these are going to be automated into the ERP system. They went to another employee and got that list and decided those tasks also need to be automated using ERP. This continued until they had a complete list of current tasks and a plan to automate them using ERP. This is a questionable approach when trying to implement technology. These organizations got little or no significant value from deploying this technology. Other organizations used a different strategy and realized that with an ERP system, they could process work in parallel instead of sequentially. With ERP they could see more data, and a lot of their data would be updated in real time. In order to take advantage of those characteristics, they redesigned their business processes, and the result was a significant benefit from implementing the technology. The same is true for AI tools. While an organization might gain some benefits from deploying AI in order to automate tasks, the true value lies in changing the way that projects are managed.

My belief is that automating specific tasks such as resource scheduling or estimating are not disruptive enough. The project management methods have to change. For example, if the project methodology changes significantly enough, there may not be a need to perform detailed estimates. However, there may be automation of tasks that could be considered disruptive because they have a significant impact on how project activities are performed. If it takes fifteen people to scan and verify a contract document but none with an AI tool, then that is significant. My concern is when project management activities are subject to a series of improvements that get in the way of making big changes. Each small improvement may total 20 percent gained in productivity, but one big change to the project methodology may result in a 40 percent increase. The other problem with task-specific productivity improvements is whether they have an impact on project success. The goal with machine learning is to increase the project success rate. Finding a new way to allocate resources might save project costs, but does it significantly increase the probability of project success?

Some published articles proclaim that AI will automate a significant amount of a project manager's tasks. That means a tool would take almost everything a project manager does now and turn it into a routine process that is repeated over and over again. Does a project manager really have that many repetitive tasks? The goal of a good project manager is to make good project decisions, and an AI tool can be used to make better decisions. The work of a project manager needs to change, but it needs to be disrupted, not automated. Once again, AI is a disruptive technology, and to get the greatest value, automating existing tasks is not the best approach.

SUMMARY

It is disturbing that major projects are constantly late and overspent, and even more disturbing is the lack of energy and determination to find a better solution. Machine learning is a new technology that offers the potential to provide amazing results as long as project stakeholders are willing to adopt it. Although there are some good AI tools that help automate project activities, doing so can take emphasis away from the true purpose of AI, which is to disrupt the project methodology. Disruption is the change needed in order to consistently deliver projects on time and on or under budget. There is no reason to be afraid of incurring worse results, since the risk of implementing AI tools for a project manager is no greater than that of any other technology, while the value can be significant. It may be seen as prudent to implement AI by using it to automate smaller pieces of the process, yet this may result in missing the greatest gain, which is changing the project methodology. Examples of disruptive AI tools are discussed later, but first there needs to be a solid understanding of the input side of machine learning algorithms, and that is project data.

CHAPTER 2

The Importance of Data

The past cannot be changed, but the future can be improved.

Data is the nourishment that feeds all software algorithms. The importance of data cannot be underestimated, and if data is managed properly, the machine learning results will provide enormous value to the organization as well as each project. Data is objective and not judgmental. A self-driving car does not evaluate the character of a person before it decides to stop and let them pass in front of the car. However, you need to have the right data accessible and in the proper format for a machine learning algorithm to function properly. The good news is that you don't need to evaluate the relevance of the data, because that is what the machine learning algorithm will do as long as the data is pertinent to project management.

AI tools work best with structured data, which is data that has been categorized, labeled, and made searchable. Data is the backbone of any system that uses a software program. The old expression used by IT people says, "Garbage in, garbage out," in reference to organizations that provide incorrect and poor-quality data and then ponder why the output does not make sense. With AI tools this is also true, although there is an additional requirement for providing a larger volume of data in order for the machine learning algorithms to be trained sufficiently to deliver an accurate result. It is incumbent on organizations and project managers to understand the preparation required as well as the expectations of adopting AI-based functionality.

GARBAGE IN

In order to train an algorithm, you need data, and there are a lot of problems around data when dealing with a machine learning tool. First, the data is typically not clean. Data fields contain typos or improperly capitalized words. Field formats are different across or sometimes within the same database. For example, a date field can be dd/mm/yy, mm/dd/yy, mm/week, yyyy/mm/dd, or any other possible permutation. There can be two data fields that actually mean the same thing and one data field that has two meanings. In one of my projects, there was a data field for an owner's name, and yet it would occasionally contain three names because there were three owners. And, of course, there is usually a column of data that contains a single data field that is supposed to have a numeric value, and it is blank. AI cannot handle blank data fields. When encountering a blank data field, the software typically lists the value as NaN, which means "not a number," and this results in an error unless steps are taken to prevent or remediate it. Should the programmer use an average of the numbers in the field, the median value, or a zero? Academics around the world are writing and publishing research papers about the best way for AI algorithms to properly handle a blank data field. It must be a serious issue.

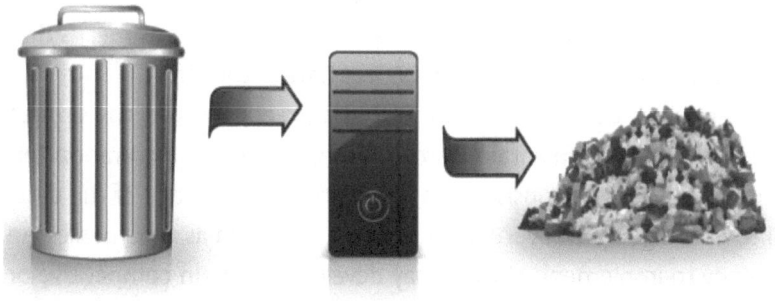

Figure 2.0

The problem with corrupt data is that it can exist in the database and not cause any serious problems. Normally, it is only when an administrator encounters the corrupt or bad data that a correction is made. When the data needs to be migrated to a new system, data issues can no longer hide, and work is required to discover the problems and correct them. Another situation is if the existing database is being accessed and used by another system and causes problems in the other system. There is normally no incentive to clean data unless there is a pressing need such as new technology or an upgrade to a new system. A business case can be made for upgrading software that uses a database, but will it include the cost and effort to clean the existing data? If not, then who is going to pay for the work? The effort needs to be sized and evaluated. Once funding is available, there are ways to get the work completed. There are contractors and contracting businesses that help with data migration by using a set of IT tools to validate the data and find anomalies. Then the business must work to remediate these, which can be very awkward and time consuming.

Some organizations hire a data architect, and part of that work is defining nomenclature or standards for critical data. Once that is complete, a validation process is used to ensure remediation is sucessful. Following that, a process needs to be implemented and adhered to in order to maintain clean data. This is a better strategy than having none. However, the volume of stored data at some organizations means that they only define a set of "critical" data as part of the effort.

How does this apply to AI tools? In a practical sense, the project manager needs to maintain historical project data in a common format and at least be consistent in the capture and storage of the data. AI tools are going to overwhelm organizations, and as time passes, an urgency to implement AI tools may develop to remain competitive or survive as an organization. In that situation, a valid business case for work to clean and structure the data would be useful, because without valid data, machine learning cannot produce accurate results.

For agile methodology, data standards will also be important, because the shorter life cycle of sprints makes it more immediately useful. Agile project sprints can use recent or streaming data to help the project stay on track.

DATA VOLUME

A large concern for organizations is, "How much data do I need?" The answer, of course, is, "It depends." In fact, data scientists and machine learning specialists are unable to determine the exact amount of data required. For a proper medical diagnosis, a lot of historical data is needed. For a self-driving car, a lot of live streaming data is required. For business models, somewhat less data is required, and it has been suggested that as few as thirty sets of data might be enough for an AI algorithm.[8]

In most but not all situations, more data will result in more accurate outcomes for prediction and classification. For large organizations this may not be an issue. For example, a government probably has a lot of project data and project results, and perhaps they even captured and stored the data. However, smaller organizations are not likely to have similar data resources when trying to use an AI tool. For example, there are a lot of associations such as a milk producers association or a country's kennel club. How do these organizations take advantage of AI tools when they are only implementing one IT project every eight to ten years? They need to collaborate. In other words, there needs to be a project management database repository where small or even medium organizations share their data. It would be strictly used to help each other take advantage of the advanced technology tools available to larger organizations.

One alternative is to simply use machine tools that are already trained. While this sounds intriguing, the results could be terrible. Imagine implementing a project to install a new email system based on machine learning tools that were trained using construction project data. This could occur when a smaller organization contracts the project implementation to a solution provider. In this situation the sponsor

---

8 Stephen Thomas, "AI and Analytics in Business," lecture, Machine Learning and Artificial Intelligence Ottawa, May 2018.

needs to ensure that the contractor has access to AI tools and a database that will be effective for their project and their organization. The issue of data availability between larger and smaller entities may create a dichotomy between successful and unsuccessful organizations as well as reputable and untrustworthy project contractors.

DATA DEPENDENCY

One of the problems with developing AI capability for project management is the diversity of the types of projects. For example, there are construction projects, software deployment projects, and projects to change business processes. While the overriding principles of project management are the same, projects in different functional areas offer a unique challenge for AI. Machine learning normally requires a significant amount of data to train the AI tool. This can be in the form of historical data such as lessons learned. However, the lessons learned from a completed construction project may not be useful for a project with the goal of deploying software. While some commonality may exist, it is more likely that an appropriate dataset from each project area is required.

The value of project management process knowledge such as that provided by PMBOK is understanding a generic set of principles that can be applied across any project. Although the principles are essential, AI requires specific details that allow an algorithm to consider relevant data in order to predict results and ultimately make an optimal decision for the project. Given this situation, the availability of good project data might be as valuable as the ability to create an algorithm that can take advantage of the data. How is your organization collecting and storing project data? In a project management survey that I conducted, 75 percent of respondents claimed that their organizations retain almost all project documents, including the budget and schedule documents. In addition, 40 percent responded that their project documents are retained forever, while 50 percent retain them for four to ten years.

Developing and using any AI tool begins with data, and that is the first significant issue. As data scientists begin to use big data, which are datasets that are too large to be handled with traditional software, it is estimated that 60 to 80 percent of their time will be spent in data cleansing tasks.[9] This includes detecting bad data, removing or correcting data, and modifying data. If a business has subjected its critical business data to data standards and adheres to those standards, then this provides a good start. With big datasets the lack of clean data means that most data fields will not move easily into an array for further analysis. The issues range from simple items, such as having a data field with data in different formats, to more complicated items, such as detecting valid or invalid data in a field.

Implementing AI and receiving the rewards is dependent on clean and manageable data. Is your organization ready to take advantage of AI tools? Probably not. The problem this creates is that the cost of generating and maintaining structured project data is likely to delay the benefits of AI technology and force the organization to seek incremental improvements instead of a game-changing advantage.

Think of a database with over a million pieces of data divided into a variety of categories. It is impossible for a human brain alone to discover similarities or dependencies in the data. A machine learning program using different classifiers is capable of doing this and is proving extremely valuable with tasks such as the interpretation and diagnosis of MRI brain scans or lung x-rays in children, because the level of accuracy is much higher than that of a skilled technician.

This concept can also be applied to project management. Specifically, how does a project manager accurately diagnose a serious

---

9 Press, "Cleaning Big Data."

project issue and make the best decision to resolve the issue? An optimal solution involves three types of data: the past, the present, and the future.

The past. AI programs rely on machine learning to use historical information for training and then make a prediction for a new set of data. For project management, the software program will look for similarities based on historical information from previous projects, such as lessons learned, and an issue log with issues, the decision, and the resulting outcome. What has occurred and was there a successful resolution? The difference between predictive analytics and a machine learning tool is that the machine learning algorithm can use a significantly larger volume of data and uncover unexpected correlations that a predictive analytics tool would not consider as part of the analysis. This is the traditional area of machine learning, which uses historical information to discover patterns and create a model.

The present. An AI tool for project management needs to also include the current project status and project environment. These can be important factors in determining the best solution to an issue or problem. PMBOK defines thirty-three project documents used to capture the project events, although not all projects maintain these documents. Large projects typically have a project schedule and capture basic information such as budget, schedule, change orders, and EVM (earned value management) metrics. The project environment may include internal factors, such as the organization's policies and procedures, as well as external factors, such as interest rates for loans, contractor prices, inflation, and resource availability. Factors in the current project environment may be required in order to assess the success rate of the various solutions or actions derived by an AI tool.

The future. The final category extends the ability of an artificial intelligence program into a different area, which is metrics about the future. What is likely to happen in the next few years or for the remaining duration of the project? This may seem like pure speculation, and that is partly true. However, both the internal and external environments exhibit trends that can be captured and used to assist in finding the best decision for project issues. Think of interest rates. In a climate where interest rates are low and inflation is beginning to climb, a rise in rates in the future can be expected. Of course, the US Federal Reserve bank and the Bank of Canada also issue statements that they expect to raise or lower rates in the future, so there is not much speculation at all. Trends such as the expected growth rates and resource availability are widely available in publications such as *The Economist* or those published by a government organization.

A project's internal environment may reveal a trend due to the inability to achieve budget targets and result in a forecast of EAC (estimate at completion) based on the CPI (cost performance index) run rate. While some results, such as the outcome of a sporting event, may be unpredictable, there are many future metrics that will easily fall within a limited set of parameters. This can be similar to predicting the path of an iceberg. It may move slightly in one direction or another, but the overall direction is very clear. The purpose of gathering all of these factors is to enhance an AI tool's ability to consider data and make accurate assessments and predictions for a project decision. A machine learning program that considers the past, present, and future will be a powerful tool to determine the best outcome in order to solve project issues.

A corpus is a body or work, and it is normally a large, structured body of texts. Examples include a movie review database with ratings or an opinion database that contains English words categorized as expressing positive or negative sentiment. The problem with the field of project management is that words can often have a different meaning in the context of a project than they have in general language. For example, if you ask a chatbot such as Siri or Alexa about a schedule, they will assume that you mean your personal calendar of appointments. In project management a schedule is a list of tasks in the project that are sequenced based on dependencies. In order to accomplish some natural language processing (NLP), there needs to be a way to interpret project management language properly.

In order to support proper decision-making strategies, there also needs to be a logic resource. For example, PMI publishes PMBOK, which has a list of tools and techniques that can be used as actions to take to find the best outcome. On the other hand, a variety of other tools and bodies of knowledge are used in project management that provide similar or even better results. Think about using a virtual assistant such as Alexa or Google Assistant and asking about a change control process for a project. The answer requires knowledge about managing a project properly. Similarly, asking if a specific task can be delayed to a different week or if resources can be shifted without a negative impact on the scheduled end date requires knowledge of the logic regarding a critical path. There is a proper and logical sequence that allows a project manager to easily answer these questions, but in addition to the data, a knowledge reference with project management logic is required.

A project status consists of a variety of metrics. Is the project on schedule? Is the budget overspent? This may include earned value management metrics (EVM). An AI program needs to access and apply these metrics in order to evaluate more of the project's current data. In addition, future project metrics are calculated, such as "Will the project end date be on schedule?" This is different than whether it is on schedule at this moment. Also, we typically try to predict whether the project will finish on or under budget, which can be very different from the current status. The logic sources for a project can help us calculate these values if they are not already part of routine project metrics that are collected and accessible to the machine learning algorithm.

This is starting to look like a lot of data gathering and retaining, so part of the work will be to determine what data needs to be retained and what data will be used and then discarded. In a machine learning program, data can be used to train the algorithm and then no longer be required unless it is being used for updates as in reinforcement learning. Similarly, there may be an opportunity to use streaming data to train a model rather than capturing and storing it.

ACCESSING THE DATA

A project management plan typically consists of a variety of documents such as a project scope statement, schedule, resource availability calendar, and risk plan. How will an AI tool access these documents? The first step is to make sure that they are stored in a common repository with clear directions to the historical documents. Each past project needs to be uniquely categorized so that they can be considered as a dataset. Text documents can be read using NLP. Excel documents can be imported into a dataframe in Python, for example, and used by the algorithm. The variety of formats such as Word, PDF, Excel, and PowerPoint make access an interesting exercise. Documents may also be stored as Google Docs or in Prezi format, which increase the locations and complexity for access. There is a high level of complexity in being able to access, read, and interpret all these project documents, which explains why AI tool developers are trying to hire so many NLP specialists.

TensorFlow is an open-source tool developed by Google. It provides an easy way to load, manipulate, and feed data to a machine learning model. Preprocessing of input data has capabilities that include normalizing a value, converting a string to an integer, and converting a floating-point number to an integer. TensorFlow can be used to handle large volumes of data more easily. Hadoop is an example of another open-source tool, and it is used for distributed processing of large datasets across clusters of connected computer servers. It can scale up to thousands of machines and is currently one of the most widely used tools for managing, storing, and processing of big data.

DATA MINING

Data mining searches for patterns and correlations in data but is not a replacement for machine learning where the data is used to train an algorithm to recognize patterns. Both technologies require access to the data, and in most cases, this is a large amount of data.

Data mining is used to analyze large databases in order to discover statistical patterns that can be used to update project documents in order to create a higher probability of project success. For the organization that has a significant amount of archived project data, a data mining tool that tries to classify the data or find anomalies is a great way to extract value from historical data. What makes a project successful in this type of organization? Are there any common factors that derailed projects where people were unable to determine what really happened? In data mining, detecting an anomaly in the data is identifying an outlier that may be interesting and require further investigation. For example, in project management it could be answering why the project was so late compared to the normal distribution of the statistical results.

Dependency modeling is another method of performing statistical searches in the data to look for relationships. A paper published by PMI that looked at timesheets found a double peak correlation: "Projects with both very low project meeting time and very high project meeting time were much more likely to have the project end up in trouble."[10]

Some organizations have vast amounts of stored project data, which could be extremely useful for training a machine learning algorithm. For machine learning, the same process is used to build a model that will be able to predict an outcome. Classification is a typical machine learning outcome, and in project management it can be used to evaluate whether a risk is likely to occur on a project, for example. An added benefit is that the machine learning tool will read that data and become trained but will not need to retain any data as part of the training. This is the way that some websites work. They don't capture website clicks attached to a user. Instead, they use the clicks to train the model with no requirement to keep the data, which results in no issues of personal privacy for the user. Other websites capture user data because they want to target that user for specific recommendations. The value in machine learning is twofold: it is unbiased in determining correlations, and it does not need to retain any information and can be an anonymous reader. In other words, you may require top secret clearance from a person to be able to view the document, but because the machine learning tool does not retain any data, it does not require the same classification. The machine learning tool simply learns from the data and does not actually remember any of the data. This is applicable to military, defense, or tax information where there is risk in having a person review the documents and discover names or improperly followed processes. With machine learning, the algorithm does not judge the sources of the data or the data content. It simply uses the data to train itself about how to make the next project successful.

---

10   C. Vandersluis, "Panning for Gold by Data-Mining Your Project Tracking Data," paper presented at PMI Global Congress 2013—North America, New Orleans, Project Management Institute, https://www.pmi.org/learning/library/project-data-mining-techniques-5854.

Organizations such as governments tend to have a lot of data and are a good source for data mining. The goal is to increase project success rates. The past cannot be changed, but the future can be improved. In order to help projects be more successful, the results need to reveal what aspects of past projects created or caused problems that led to an unsuccessful outcome. There may be small improvements discovered as part of data mining, but the objective is to discover a significant cause of project delays and budget overruns. Higher success rates start with ensuring that a project has comprehensive project management plans and a proper strategy that will result in a successful project. After uncovering the causes by using data mining, adjustments can be made to future projects in order to avoid similar problems. The next step is to develop and implement an AI tool that can be trained to ensure that the project starts well and remains on track to achieve the project outcome.

HOW TO PREPARE THE DATA

What can you do as a project manager or part of a PMO to get ready for AI tools? If data is so important, where do you start? The best course of action is to ensure that there is a repository for the data that you already capture. In most projects this should be the project scope statement, all change orders, lessons learned, and a list of issues or problems that had to be resolved typically as a result of a status meeting.

The scope statement can reveal the detail or depth of complexity of the project. Some scope statements are small, while others can be hundreds of pages. The change requests are normally logged, and then some are accepted, becoming a change order, and some are rejected or deferred. It is important to save the change orders details as well, as these may reflect on the original scope or simply environmental changes that require additional work.

The lessons learned document needs to be a formal document that provides a level of detail for the project. A statement that "resources were inadequate" is not as helpful as documenting the gap, such as the true level of resources required and any other considerations such as training or availability. A structured lessons learned document can be used as input for a number of potential AI tools. While documents such as the scope statement may be acceptable in the current form, the lessons learned for both successful and challenging projects is likely to require more structured format as well as details that are not currently captured. For example, a typical lessons learned issue will result in an action item to resolve the issue for future projects. This might be an update to an organization policy or a new communication requirement. However, the additional data should be captured if the action item succeeded in achieving the result desired or if the same issue returns in other projects.

A project status meeting can uncover a variety of issues or problems that need to be resolved. Two simple examples are when a training course does not include a key requirement or a team member is unavailable at a required time. An action item is taken with a due date and an assigned person responsible, and similar to the lessons learned, the issues log needs to capture the data if the action is successful. The importance of the issues log is that it is a snapshot of the project as it progresses toward the due dates. Most project data will be historical data, and while the issues data is also historical, it has a current aspect to it that makes it more useful.

Table 2: Typical Sample Issues Report

#	Issue	Description	Assigned	Due date	Resolution
1	Training course gap	The training course does not include data maintenance	Paul	23 Mar	Renegotiated with contractor to include the additional content
2	Resource shortage	Khalid is unavailable for the next two weeks	Chris	20 Feb	Acquired a replacement on loan from another project

Table 3: Typical Sample Issues Report for Machine Learning

#	Issue	Description	Assigned	Due date	Resolution	Impact on budget	Impact on schedule
1	Training course gap	The training course does not include data maintenance	Paul	23 Mar	Renegotiated with contractor to include the additional content	$20,000	2 days
2	Resource shortage	Khalid is unavailable for the next two weeks	Chris	20 Feb	Acquired a replacement on loan from another project	None	None

Deploying a successful machine learning model requires the right data. Projects managers can work with IT staff to ensure the data being used is a good fit for the model. This is not meant to be a restriction of what the machine learning tool should access, because that might make it less accurate. The data needs to fit within the project parameters for the tool being used.

Someone in the organization needs to take responsibility for data management for projects. This includes creating or maintaining a repository that can be accessed by a variety of AI tools and yet still retain security around personal or proprietary data. The following are important aspects of being able to use project management data.

Structure the data. Fairly simple changes can be implemented to make the data more understandable. For example, with an issues log, the data can be structured so that the type of issue is identified. Is it a scope issue or resource issue? Create specific categories and use them across the documents. A scope issue should be related to a specific section in the scope statement document. The same is true for the risk register. The risks should be linked to activities that relate to the project plan and in the scope statement. It sounds like a lot more work, but in reality, it is simply being better organized and will help everyone understand the interconnections in the project.

For the overall project, a judgment on success needs to be defined. What makes this project successful from a *project* point of view? Did it meet the requirements for budget and schedule? This judgment helps by creating a label for the project, which is essential for supervised learning.

One of the distinctions that needs to be made is whether the project met the customer's expectations. That is important but not necessarily the goal of AI tools. AI tools are increasing the probability of the project process. In many cases that will result in both project success and a customer recognition of success. However, there may be circumstances where the project is completed, and the project outcome is no longer aligned or effective for the customer's original objective. It may be possible for an AI tool to monitor and correlate data from the external environment in order to include this as a probability factor for meeting customer expectations.

Maintain data integrity. Once project data is structured, it needs to be made consistent across all projects in the organization. This might be easy for some organizations but will be difficult for others. If a PMO exists that can enforce a level of standards, that will be helpful. Otherwise each project manager needs to follow a template and adhere to standards.

Store the project data. Each completed project with all the completed documents needs to be stored in an accessible repository. Project closure normally is the process where this type of work is done. However, in my experience it is also the stage where everyone is happy that the project is complete, and time pressures may prevent effective work. The euphoria of project completion is followed by the tedious administrative work of project closure. We need to find a way to ensure proper data retention for project data.

It may be possible to train the algorithm with the data as it occurs or immediately after the project has ended, which alleviates the need to store data. Professor Angelov from the University of Lancaster has performed research on how machine learning tools can take streaming data as input and process that into a model that can produce results.[11] This poses the question of whether the data needs to be stored or if it is sufficient to feed the data directly to a machine learning tool in order to provide what can be called real-time training.

From an overall IT perspective, in a large organization, there needs to be a plan for the scope of machine learning tools and sufficient capacity and flexibility that fit into your current organization's data strategy. Data standards need to be determined unless they are already in place and being adhered to. With more than one AI tool,

---

11 Plamendon Angelov, "Autonomous Learning for Autonomous Systems," lecture, Machine Learning and Artificial Intelligence Ottawa, September 2018.

an infrastructure design may be required. As each new tool becomes available, the data approach needs to be comprehensive and not short-sighted or fragmented. Also, the data flow needs to be understood so that it flows easily without obstacles or restrictions. Ideally all the project documents are included in the database.

In the design of the system, there may be a need to evaluate and determine whether it is appropriate to use a data platform such as TensorFlow or an equivalent that is capable of increasing data storage reliably and in a cost-effective way. An on-premise or cloud solution also needs to be considered. There are many factors to evaluate in this decision, and it will most likely be dictated by the organization's data strategy.

The challenge with introducing new technology in projects is that every project is unique. However, all projects follow some common basic processes and require the creation of project documents. One possible application for an AI tool is to search for anomalies across project documents to verify completeness, accuracy, and coherence in the project plan. Another application is to use lessons learned documents to allow an AI tool to predict where the project will likely have problems, suggest why the problems are likely to occur, and describe the ensuing impact on the project scope, budget, and schedule. Imagine having a project management aid that performs analyses with results that easily increase project success rates.

One advantage of an AI tool is that the number, size, and complexity of the documents are not impediments to success. A disadvantage of current project documents is that for a project to be successful, the documents may need to be connected. This means the inclusion of tags to indicate linkages across all documents as opposed to independent documents, which may contain abstract or generic references. Especially at this early stage of AI tools, NLP will not be able to understand that a specific risk is linked to a number of tasks. It might not even understand that a quality measurement is linked to a project's deliverable defined in the scope document.

Table 4: Sample Project Activity List

Act. ID	Activity
1	Define process
2	Create data map
3	Create test cases
4	Configure processes
5	Perform user review
6	Perform configuration

Table 5: Sample Project Risk List

Description	Owner	Response strategy	Activity ID link
Risk 1	Risk owner 1	Response strategy 1	3, 4
Risk 2	Risk owner 2	Response strategy 2	4

A machine learning algorithm might be able to learn the linkages from historical data, but only where events occurred that illustrated the actual linkages. The links in tables 4 and 5 provide a simple illustration of how it can be accomplished and are not representative of all linkages in a project. There are many others, such as resources and quality requirements, and some may not be linked directly to a specific activity. Numbered links in the data to clarify these connections will be an important mechanism for AI tools to successfully crawl through project data and extrapolate issues that require adjustments in order to optimize the performance of the project.

In project management, project documents are not clean and easy to read. It is fairly straightforward to use NLP to read a document if it is in Word or PDF. Then the machine learning tool uses logic to perform classification or prediction. It is more complicated to read a project schedule, for example. Additional logic is required to understand the meaning of a critical path and be able to interpret the sequence and dependencies. Can the tool invoke the critical path chart and look for the red line? Once the complexity of access and interpretation is solved, then it needs to calculate float, free float, and then look at resource loading. Implementing AI for interpreting a project schedule will require an expert system first and then an overlay of machine learning. To have a complete picture of the project, other factors that interact with the schedule, such as risk and quality, also need to be considered. The complexity of reading a schedule includes understanding the task dependencies, critical path, and possibly EVM metrics as well as how the schedule interacts with the other aspects of the project such as quality and risk.

While the machine learning part might be the most exciting, it is part of the system, and this is especially true if there is a large database with a variety of project information. There needs to be a data collection stage or a step that provides access to the data. There needs to be a data verification process that ensures the data is structured, and from that data the features or critical elements to be used by the machine learning tool need to be identified. Once the machine learning results are produced, there may need to be further analysis, or at least a procedure needs to be in place for how the results are going to be used.

Smaller organizations that have insufficient or unrelated data for a specific project are at a disadvantage. If an organization initiates one project in five years, not only is there not enough data, but there is not likely to be consistency in the structure of the project documents. Also, if organizations such as associations are collaborating by sharing project documents in order to train a machine learning algorithm, it will be unlikely that the documents have a consistent structure. They are at a distinct disadvantage unless they find a way to create common templates with similar organizations. Otherwise AI tools will make larger organizations more effective and leave smaller organizations and associations to their own results. Another option is for vendors to offer a trained algorithm to the smaller organizations. The problem with this type of arrangement will be if a generically trained algorithm can be used across a number of different organizations with any degree of success.

When building predictive models and eventually tools using artificial intelligence for project management, lack of data is a serious issue. Insufficient data in a machine learning model causes a problem known as underfitting. There is simply not enough data for an algorithm to properly learn the correlations and create an accurate model, which results in inaccurate predictions. Also, the model itself may be too simple and require a more complex algorithm. A truly successful model should consist of more than historical data and include current project data or any results that provide feedback into the model. Feedback provides continuous improvement of the prediction's accuracy. Overfitting is the creation of a model that attempts to match the data too closely. This is a situation where there are outliers that should be ignored, but the machine learning algorithm tries to include them as part of the model. The result is a model that may not predict future observations accurately.

SUMMARY

AI tools need data in order to produce valuable results. Project management tends to focus on delivering a successful project and not learning how to store useful data. Therefore, a change is required so that structured data standards are specified and followed for project management data. The IT group and project managers need to work together to deliver a benefit for future projects in the organization. For large project-based organizations, there needs to be an IT infrastructure that manages both data and AI tools, and this typically includes decisions about using local servers or accessing the cloud, data architecture, data capture polices, and more. For small and medium organizations, the problem will be finding sufficient project data to train algorithms that can produce results for their specific projects. Using AI tools will be a valuable opportunity for project management. However, it starts with being able to feed the tools with data, and that may require a lot of work before the organization is ready. The next section describes a series of potential machine learning tools and how they will improve project success rates. This will be the exciting part, although after learning about the potential of the tools, it will be good to think about the data required in order for them to produce accurate results.

CHAPTER 3
Sample AI Tools

AI is a disruptive technology. In order to get the value, you need to change the way that you manage projects.

This section is meant to challenge the way you manage projects as well as provoke thought processes about how to use AI to change your project methodology. It is about applying AI to project management, and the main focus is on AI tools intended to improve project success rates. Some will be disruptive and change the way projects are managed, and some will provide significant efficiency improvements to one aspect of project management that needs it.

It is common to read sensational headlines such as "AI funding in 2018 was $20 billion," but the reality is that the funding needs to be applied correctly in order to solve the most pressing problems, and very little to none of that was applied directly to project management.[12] Another challenge regarding AI tools that is common with other software is how to optimize or get the most value out of the AI tools that are implemented. It's similar to Microsoft Word where everyone uses on average about ten to twenty menu items, and yet there are over a hundred available. With AI tools for project management, there will be common uses, but taking full advantage of the capability means being creative and finding those extra features that will truly work for your organization to increase project success rates. Finding and taking advantage of a capability that appears buried in the tool can provide significant improvement beyond what was expected when the software was acquired.

PREDICTING PROJECT SUCCESS

Wouldn't it be great if you had a tool that could accurately predict the success of a project before it starts? The resources and energy saved by preventing a doomed project would certainly be valuable, but even

---

12   Arne Holst, "Artificial Intelligence (AI) Funding Worldwide Cumulative Through March 2019, By Category," Statista, May 8, 2019, https://www.statista.com/statistics/943136/ai-funding-worldwide-by-category/.

more valuable is making sure that every project starts with a high probability of success. This is one of the ways that AI tools can have an impact on project management processes. A project success predictor tool calculates the probability of success for a project before it begins based on a review of the project management documents created for project implementation. Typically, an AI predictor tool is a software program consisting of an algorithm that uses a neural network to correlate patterns in the data using a supervised learning model. The data is provided from a series of historical projects with a set of data captured for each project. The projects are labeled "success" or "failure" as defined by the user. The AI tool is trained using historical data, analyzes the project planning documents for a newly proposed project, and then calculates a probability of success based on the model created from the training data.

The machine learning algorithm uses data to create a regression analysis that forecasts the probability of project success based on any variety of factors used for input to the algorithm. Why would you start to implement a project that has a low probability of success? The capability of an AI-based prediction algorithm can make it a powerful tool for project managers, project sponsors, and the PMO. Below is a description of a basic algorithm that uses historical data, and this is followed by an intriguing feature of adding current metrics. Adoption of this type of tool will change project management processes.

The Predictor Tool

A predictor tool consists of three components: the input data, the software containing the machine learning algorithm, and the output. The input data is typically a number of factors based on historical projects completed by an organization or within an industry. Each project is labeled as "successful" or "not successful." This can be user defined for an organization or determined as the condition of delivering the project scope, with no more than 5 percent over budget or 5 percent late to the scheduled end date, for example. It assumes that the quality requirements defined in the scope document remain constant and that risk factors can still have an impact on finances or schedule. Since the projects are labeled, the algorithm is trained using a supervised model. The algorithm consists of a mathematical model such as a neural network. In my research, alternative algorithms such as support vector machines (SVM) and random forest were tried, but a neural network produced the most consistent and accurate results. The output of the neural network is a probability of success. The tool uses the inputs to train the AI algorithm for correlations in the data that are not possible for a human brain to understand. It is these correlations that result in a probability prediction.

How much data is required for a predictor tool to make accurate predictions? The answer can be determined by research and testing and may be variable based on the type of organization or project. This is a problem that data scientists continue to work on. As mentioned previously in chapter 2, the medical field requires more data to increase the probability of an accurate diagnosis. In business the requirement can be somewhat less. For project management, this is one of the areas that require a lot more testing. There is likely a range of datasets that are adequate, and we are currently unsure about those amounts.

Some organizations consistently maintain a project database for current and historical projects that is extensive enough to use as input for a machine learning tool. Other organizations do not understand the value of project data as it relates to the process for implementing projects. This is something that needs to change. All organizational data is valuable, and increasing project success rates will depend on capturing more data that can help improve the project methodology.

As described in chapter 2, there are implications of too little data and inaccurate models. Training a machine learning tool with insufficient data causes underfitting, which decreases the accuracy of the prediction. Overfitting skews the model by trying to fit in outliers. As prediction tools become common and provide value for organizations, the amount of data and more accurate models will be tuned based on using test data and becoming experienced in understanding how the model works. However, any model used for accurate predictions still depends on the input data.

Project Screening and Selection
The project screening process normally consists of a set of criteria used to screen out unsuitable projects. For example, the financial benefit may be too low or the time period for implementation too long. The screening factors can be unique to an organization or common across most projects. Calculating the probability of success for a project can be a common standard for project screening.

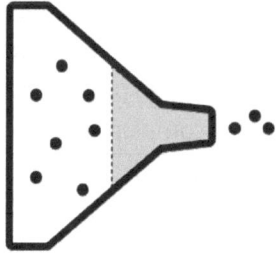

Figure 3.0

Looking at this from a different perspective, the screening process provides threshold values for projects to receive further consideration in the process. The good part about using a predictor tool at this stage is that all projects are evaluated to the same standard. If one project receives a 72 percent probability of success, and the second project receives a 95 percent probability of success, then one project has a clear advantage. The organization will determine what probability is the hurdle to overcome for the projects that will move forward for further consideration.

The project selection process aims to select the best project from a number of alternatives. There can be many factors to consider, such as the financial and strategic value of each project. However, the addition of a metric such as the probability of success adds a layer of confidence to achieve the objectives supported by the strategic and financial benefits. The factor can be included in a weighted scoring model to select the best project, although it is more likely that the factor needs to be considered as a standalone item that is subject to more scrutiny, as will be seen in an example in the next section.

Of course, you are likely to select a project that has a success probability of 95 percent instead of a project that a has a success probability of 65 percent. However, what if you absolutely must implement the project that has a 65 percent probability? It may be for legal, regulatory, or strategic reasons that this project is required. What is the next step when faced with this result? Logically, the project manager would gather the project team and rework the project planning documents. In reality this means the strategy. As project managers we are planners, and we know that more work completed to create a successful plan will result in an easier implementation. Perhaps there is something missing in the documentation, or perhaps the strategy is all wrong. Whatever the issue, the planning for this project needs to be improved in order to achieve a higher probability of success before the project begins. This is not a simulation tool, so the predictor will not automatically tell you what area needs to be improved. Most project managers, on seeing such a poor probability of success, are likely to quickly identify areas that are weak or where the project plan needs to have a better strategy.

Table 6: Using a Project Outcome Success Predictor in Project Initiation

Process	Purpose	AI predictor tool usage
Project screening	Projects must meet a threshold or are eliminated	Include the success probability result as one of the screening criteria
Project selection	The "best" projects are selected among alternatives that have passed the screening process	Include success probability as a factor for consideration
Mandatory project	Project must proceed due to legal, regulatory, or strategic reasons	Increase the probability of success by reviewing and upgrading the planning documents and implementation strategy

Predictions During Project Execution

While a probability of success before the project begins may offer an improvement to project success rates, there are enhancements that will make this type of tool even more useful, possibly invaluable. Imagine a tool that can be used as the project is executed to determine if the probability of success is increasing or decreasing.

How useful is such a tool? Pretend you are in a video game called project management. You are at the start of a long hallway that has doors on both sides. You walk along the hallway then turn to your right and open a door. You run the predictor tool, and it indicates that the probability of success for your project has now dropped to 45 percent. You close the door and walk further down the hallway, turning to a door on the left. You open the door and run the predictor tool. It indicates that your project now has a 98 percent probability of success. What is happening? As a project manager, you now have an AI tool helping and supporting your decision-making process in order to increase and maintain a high probability of success for your project to the very end.

What data will be required? It starts with identifying and collecting specific project metrics as the project is executed. This includes factors such as earned value management metrics as well as factors on which the project was approved, such as return on investment or payback period. In addition, environmental factors can be collected, including external factors such as the rate of inflation, bank lending rate, or the duration it takes to acquire resources. The data collected may also include future metrics such as expected growth of the organization, the expected price of commodities, and economic forecast data. AI requires a lot of data and can determine correlations that we are unable to derive. Of course, for some organizations the cost and ability to collect the data needs to be considered as well.

Once the factors are determined, an AI tool can classify the trends as helpful to the project, meaning an increased probability of success, or detrimental to the project, meaning a decreased probability of success. In addition, specific project decisions can be classified as part of a successful result or part of a negative result. There are many other ways to use a predictor tool. That's the advantage of understanding and adopting an AI tool. It can be flexible to meet your needs wherever you decide to install it in the project processes. AI can decipher data in a way that we cannot, and it is to our advantage to use this technology to complete more projects successfully.

Using a Predictor Tool in a Gating Process

Some organizations use a "gate" process to divide projects into distinct phases or stages. The gates are clearly defined milestones achieved when all the tasks required by each milestone are complete. A typical example is design-test-release. The gate also becomes a review and decision point in the project. This allows an organization to carefully review the project's progress and accomplishments. In addition, a gate normally has a checklist that must be complete to allow the project to proceed to the next stage. This is a control point for several concerns, such as funding, quality, risk, and schedule. So how does a predictor tool help?

There is a perplexing occurrence where a project arrives at a gate, passes the checklist, and then fails miserably during the next stage. This is a cause for indescribable frustration. The predictor tool can help in a couple of ways. First, it is possible that the checklist does not contain all the data elements necessary for the project to complete the next stage successfully. After all, it normally consists of completed tasks. Has the risk increased since the start of the project, or what anomalies might have occurred? The predictor tool can analyze historical data from projects and make a judgment as to the probability of passing the next gate. The second way a predictor tool can be used in this situation is to consider the factors that the project will face in the next stage and correlate that data into a higher or lower probability of success if the project proceeds. This is also the point where modifications can be made to the project plan in order to increase the probability of success for the project.

Table 7: Using AI in a Gate Process

Process	Purpose	AI predictor tool usage
Phase or stage gate	Complete a checklist and make a decision to allow the project to continue	• Consider historical data to predict the probability of success • Use current metrics and environmental data up to the next gate to predict the probability of success

Observation
Predictions will reflect the culture and success of the organization. An AI tool will not resolve poorly designed and poorly executed projects. It will only confirm that they will fail. An organization that has a good

structure, has clear project processes, and captures project data consistently is likely to be more successful in adopting a predictor tool and using it successfully.

One of the problems in creating a prediction tool is the lack of good data. What business will readily provide data for projects that have not been successfully completed? Also, many organizations consider their project data to be proprietary, and perhaps some may even consider their project implementation processes a critical success factor. Of course, that assumes that they are consistently successful with project implementation, something rare in most organizations. As mentioned previously, machine learning algorithms for project management face a lack of data, which results in the problem known as underfitting. There is simply not enough data for an algorithm to properly learn the correlations and subsequently make accurate predictions. Also, the model itself may be too simple and require a more complex algorithm. A truly successful model should consist of more than historical data. It should include current project data or any results that provide feedback that offers a continuous improvement of prediction accuracy.

In addition, there will be external factors that are difficult to quantify, such as the hiring of contractors or acquiring a vendor to deliver the project. The ability and adequacy of contractors can be considered a risk and added to the risk factors included with the data being fed to the predictor algorithm. In the situation of issuing a request for proposal (RFP), one of the criteria can be for the vendor to include predictor results based on their plan. There are no easy solutions to external factors and the lack of data, especially at the earlier stages of AI for project management.

It is too presumptuous to determine whether projects need to be organized by common factors such as function or objective rather than having a single algorithm that fits all projects. Will we need to resort to building models of AI that fit only subsets of projects, such as construction, software implementation, or business process redesign projects?

It is unlikely that a "super" predictor can determine accurate results for all projects. Perhaps the algorithm will be the same, but at the very least, the input data needs to be more appropriate to the project.

A Very Simple Predictor Example

As part of my research, I worked with a number of college students to build an AI predictor tool. Data was collected from thirty-five real projects that were labeled as successes or failures. Across the project management plan documents for a project, multiple factors from each document were identified and considered to be the most significant. This was verified by a survey of project managers. There were eighty-seven factors from each project, and these were used for input into the predictor algorithm. The factors for each project were identified in binary format. In other words, if a project contained the factor in the plan, it was considered a 1; if not, a 0. The machine learning model was created as a three-layer neural network. An example of user interface for a sample predictor tool is shown in figure 3.1.

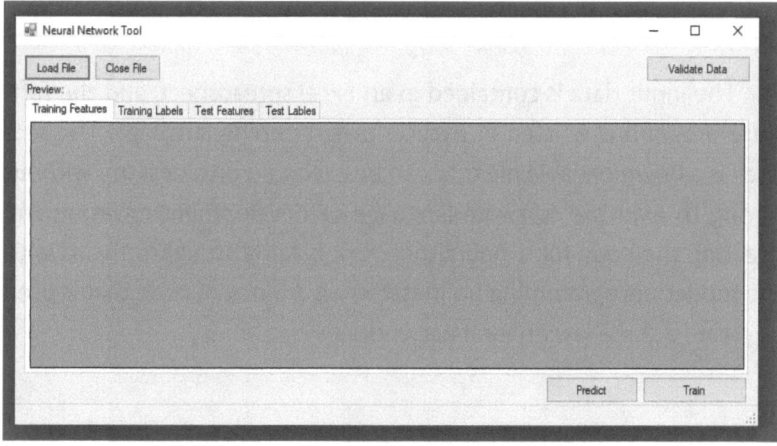

Figure 3.1

Once the algorithm was trained with the historical data, the software was tested against projects that had known results. After this verification stage, the data from a new project was used as input, and the output was a probability of success in a percentage format for that project. A graphical representation of a single-layer neural network is shown in figure 3.2.

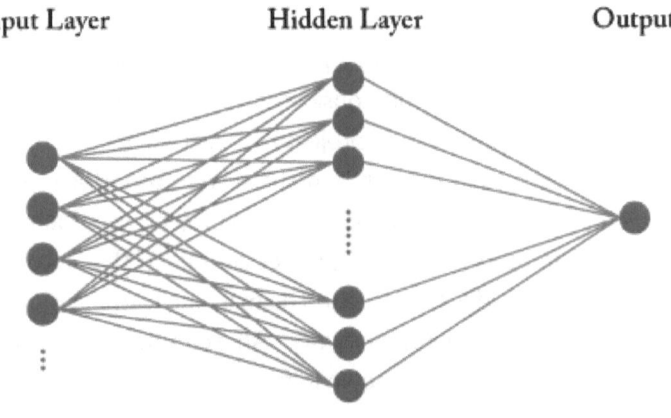

Figure 3.2

The input data is contained in an Excel spreadsheet, and the software program is written in Python programming language. The tool itself is a downloadable file that can be executed on a desktop without having to load the software language or development environment. Creating the code for a neural network is fairly straightforward with the modern programming utilities. Here is a block of code that is used to create a three-layer neural network.

```
# create model
model = Sequential()
model.add(Dense(87, input_dim=87, activation='relu'))
model.add(Dense(42, activation='relu'))
model.add(Dense(12, activation='relu'))
model.add(Dense(1, activation='sigmoid'))
```

Building an AI Predictor Tool for Project Management

A data flow architecture is similar to looking inside a building and seeing how it works. For IT applications it normally shows data inputs, how the data is processed, and then the outputs. A typical data flow for the predictor tool is shown in figure 3.3.

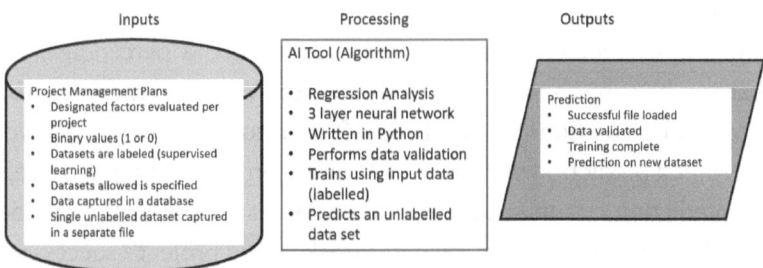

Figure 3.3

Inputs. For the training process, the predictor tool receives access to the project management plan documents and uses NLP to identify whether the factors are present. If the factor is found, then a 1 is added to the appropriate data field. If not, a 0 is entered. Since the projects are labeled as success or failure, a 1 is used to indicate success, and a 0 is used to indicate a project designated as not successful. The historical data is divided with several labeled sets being used as test data to ensure that the model functions accurately. Any number of projects are allowed for training, although there should be a determination of what number is too high or what number of projects is insufficient for training purposes.

Processing. The input data is loaded and validated to ensure that there are no blank data fields and that the data is formatted properly. This is performed for training data and test data as well as the unlabeled data that is the subject of a prediction. Through a number of tests of the training and test data, a neural network was determined as the most accurate algorithm to use. More work can be done to check any variability of the predictions by changing the number of layers of the neural network. The basic process for a machine learning tools is train, test, and predict. This is a perfect example of this process.

Outputs. Once training is complete and verified with test data, the new project prediction is produced. The result is a percentage, and that can be subject to further interpretation. What are the limits to a successful prediction? Is 95 percent sufficient to proceed? How do you interpret a prediction of 78 percent? For the project screening process, the prediction factors should at least be comparable since they are derived from common historical data. Tracking the project's success will result in more credibility as well as provide feedback to improve the accuracy of the tool. The number of factors identified in the planning documents is not fixed and can be expanded to include a large amount of data if this improves the prediction accuracy.

The Future of a Predictor Tool

Predicting project success is actually very difficult. There are so many variables and so many factors that can go wrong in a project. Is it really possible? I believe so. We see complexity in every project, and every project is unique. Yet experienced project managers will tell you when they have an intuitive feeling that an issue is going to derail the project. It might be poor communication, improperly evaluated risks, or unanticipated client change requests. But if the same issues appear consistently, it should be obvious that a software program can be trained to identify similar situations and predict a similar result.

The predictor tool of the future will be fully integrated with an organization's data. That includes historical projects, policies and procedures, strategic direction, and financial objectives. The predictor tool will not tell you what projects to implement to make the organization more successful, but it will tell you if the strategy and plan created for a project will be successful. The predictor tool will be seamless, interfacing with all the required data, whether that is internal to the organization on their database or external using the internet to capture environmental data. Project planning and execution documents will be read using NLP, which will capture the values required for the machine learning algorithm. Perhaps the tools will also accept live streaming data from the project as it progresses. Above all, there needs to be a feedback loop that captures data and updates the model on a regular basis.

Will a tool like this change the way you manage projects? The biggest challenge will be for the project stakeholders to believe the prediction probability results and commit to taking appropriate action to achieve success. That includes accepting changes to the project methodology and then adapting to further changes as the AI tools become more advanced and significantly more accurate.

AI FOR STAKEHOLDER MANAGEMENT

This section is about using natural language processing (NLP) and sentiment analysis to make a project manager much more effective at communicating and managing people. The focus is on the project team and other stakeholders, people in the organization who have a vested interest in the project.

As project managers we are constant targets for training courses. Are you a good leader? Do you want to be a better communicator? There are a lot of courses about managing teams. From emotional intelligence to communicating effectively, it seems to be an endless challenge to improve ourselves so that we can be better people and interact better with other people. I'm not sure what is going on in projects, but in life I talk to people every day, and we seem to all get along well. When someone receives a task with a deadline, it creates pressure, and then different personalities flare up. The project manager needs to understand the best way to manage all those different people. Beyond the project team, there are other project stakeholders, and it would be great to know exactly how to communicate with everyone. An AI tool can distinguish the variety of personalities and become a valuable assistant for the project manager.

Deciphering Language with NLP
Natural language processing is used to create models that allow a computer to interact with a human using language. When a human speaks or creates written text such as an instant message or an email, it is called an utterance. One of the difficult aspects is to ensure that the context of utterances is compared to project management vocabulary. There are terms in project management that have a different meaning from general speech. Determining a positive or negative sentiment with regard to a project environment is challenging, because project management has a subset of language with its own nuances.

NLP can also be used to uncover utterances that reveal whether the threshold levels of stakeholders is in jeopardy. In other words, the project status in terms of a late schedule, for example, can be above the tolerance level for the project sponsor, who has the authority to demand a budget review or ask for a justification of the project or reconsideration of the appropriate project manager to implement the project. Given this type of problem, the project manager needs to be creative in order to resolve the issue, although if historical project data contains a similar situation, then the project manager may check the AI algorithm for the best possible solution.

How Sentiment Analysis Helps the Project Manager

Sentiment analysis is derived from machine learning algorithms and is typically used in recommender systems to suggest what books or movies you might like. It is based on your personal preferences and reviews by users.

For project management this can be applied in a number of ways:

1. An analysis of documents such as a scope statement can be performed to determine whether they are likely to result in a positive or negative project outcome. This is accomplished by using classification similar to classifying images. The method is to assess scope statements for successful projects and compare them to scope statements that have caused significant project problems. While it may seem obvious to an experienced project manager who identifies gaps in a document, a machine learning algorithm has superior capability. How much detail from previous projects and documents can a project manager remember? A machine learning algorithm can input and analyze hundreds or even thousands of previous projects and is able to identify key elements that are likely to create project problems.

2. An analysis of organizational emails and instant messages can be done to evaluate whether project sentiment is favorable

or unfavorable. This can be used as a feedback mechanism to evaluate the effectiveness of project communication.

3. An analysis of organizational emails and instant messages can be done in order to verify or change actions used to manage project stakeholders. This is certainly an area of controversy with possible privacy concerns. However, this is about what is possible, not what may or may not be ethical. An organization may decide that any content that uses internal computer systems should be available for access by AI software programs. A sentiment analysis tool can detect changes in the level of stakeholder engagement and recommend corrective actions. This can provide valuable information for a project manager who receives early feedback that a stakeholder who was positive has now turned resistant to project implementation. These are only a few of the possibilities for sentiment analysis in project management. The availability of these tools is imminent, and organizations will be challenged to decide how they will be used.

AI Tools Based on Sentiment Analysis and More

Every project has numerous stakeholders, from team members to customers and other people in the organization who have a vested interested in the project outcome. And among all those stakeholders, there are truly annoying ones. Yes, there are stakeholders who want your project to fail or somehow make you look bad. This is the life of a project manager who must find a way to be successful within a politicized organization. There are also stakeholders who have legitimate concerns as the project makes progress, and they often have threshold limits, for example, to the amount of risk, potential cost overruns, or delays in the completion date. In all these situations, an AI tool for managing stakeholders will be valuable for both resolving problems and reducing the stress level of the project manager and the project team. Of course, there are supportive stakeholders and ones who promote the project objectives with enthusiasm. A good AI tool to manage stakeholders will suggest the best way to communicate with all stakeholders regardless of their attitude toward the project.

The purpose of an AI tool for stakeholder management is to help the project manager proactively manage stakeholder concerns. It also allows the project manager to be more effective in communicating with stakeholders since the AI tool can match the best communication style for each stakeholder based on their personality profile.

There are three major components to this type of algorithm. The first is an assessment of the stakeholders, which includes their personality type and any threshold or tolerance limits. These can be determined easily outside the algorithm but can also be assessed with AI tools more commonly used for marketing to individuals. The second component is sentiment analysis, which uses a variety of sources that are directly produced by the stakeholder, such as emails or instant messages, and performs an assessment of positive, negative, or neutral feeling toward the project or a specific aspect of the project. Finally, given a proper assessment on sentiment, the project manager will receive guidance on communicating effectively. With a Myers-Briggs personality profile, for example, the best way to communicate with an extrovert is not always the best way to communicate with an introvert. If a stakeholder is highly negative, the project manager can take action to diffuse an issue before it becomes more serious.

Story: Understanding Coworker Interactions
John was a coworker who was brilliant in his own way but was most effective when he thought about a problem for a while before talking about it. However, that was not his normal style. If you approached him

and raised an issue, he would express an answer immediately regardless of how simplistic or complex the solution might be. To get the most out of John's intelligence, we developed a "hit-and-run" office strategy for him. Whenever we had an issue and needed John's input, we would walk up to his desk, tell him the problem, then immediately walk away before he could respond, claiming that we were late for a meeting or giving another excuse. It worked amazingly well. Given time to analyze and reflect, he developed a more comprehensive perspective and proposed great solutions. Communicating with individuals can be very complex, and you always want it to be effective.

There are times when I wish I had the tool described here. I had an employee working on a project who appeared to be under severe mental stress. The stress was not due to project issues, and he did not let it affect his performance. He was a brilliant mathematician and solid worker. The stress was external to the work environment. Nonetheless any potential changes to his responsibilities increased his anguish. In hindsight, with this type of tool, I might have been better at communicating with him. There are times when you wish you knew the exact words to say in situations, and eventually you might learn this over time. An AI tool can help you know what to say for every situation.

Building a Stakeholder Management Tool
A typical data flow for a stakeholder management tool is shown in figure 3.4.

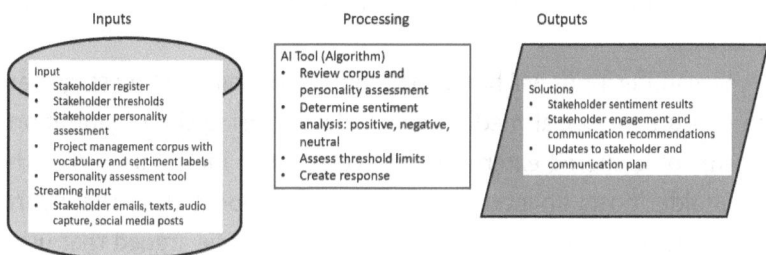

Figure 3.4

Inputs. The inputs start with the stakeholder register with categorizations such as position in the organization, level of influence over the project, and desired role in the project. Next is a document that contains the analysis of the stakeholder threshold limits, which includes items such as the budget, schedule, risk, and quality. If possible, it includes probable reactions to exceeding the stakeholder's threshold level in any of these areas. For example, a project sponsor might become agitated if the project exceeds the threshold level for funding. As the project progresses, the overspending on tasks can be much greater than a threshold level, so the stakeholder may request action and a more detailed review of the project with regard to future expectations.

The input may also contain a stakeholder personality assessment. Stakeholders can submit to a personality assessment such as Myers-Briggs, or a software program can assess the personalities based on a series of text documents such as emails. Third-party personality assessment tools are readily available that create a profile based on personal emails, texts, social media profiles, or any documents you create.[13] There also needs to be a project management vocabulary that can be used to understand the language of project stakeholders. Project language has some unique words and phrases that are not easily understood outside

---

13 Apply Magic Sauce, https://applymagicsauce.com/, University of Cambridge.

of a project context. This makes sentiment analysis algorithms more accurate.

Streaming input will be the stakeholder's emails, text messages, audio capture, or social media posts collected using the organization's systems or gathered externally by accessing the information that the stakeholder posts on internet sites. This presupposes that the organization allows an AI tool to access the data. It can be argued that using the organization's servers for email and text messaging, for example, means that any content belongs to the organization and is therefore not a privacy issue.

Table 8: Sample Stakeholder Register

Stakeholder	Role	Title	Expectations	Impact/ power	Threshold or tolerance limits

Note: This is a typical stakeholder register, although it may be different depending on the project and the organization.

Table 9: Sample Stakeholder Register Fields That Can Be Used by an AI Tool

Stakeholder	Personality type	Current sentiment	Previous sentiment

Processing. The main component is a sentiment analysis algorithm, which uses NLP to determine whether a stakeholder communication is positive or negative toward the project or project manager. The input in the form of text or utterances is analyzed for sentiment, and the algorithm uses both the personality assessment and threshold limits in the stakeholder register before preparing a response or reaction.

The project management corpus is a valuable source of content that is needed in order to perform an accurate analysis of the utterances.

Outputs. The output is a recommended response to the stakeholder that can be made electronically or in person by the project manager if the issue is serious and the tool suggests that course of action. If the sentiment is considered neutral, no action may be required. For negative sentiment a recommended action is given to the project manager about how to engage and communicate with the stakeholder based on their personality. This is the ability to influence the stakeholder in the most effective way. If successful, the project manager may need to update the communication plan or the stakeholder characteristics in the stakeholder register.

Story: Risk Threshold
When I worked in the technology industry, we had a project pushing the limits of the existing technology. After only four months into the two-year project, the project sponsor decided to cancel it, citing too many risks. It was a new process technology, a new packaging technology, and a new product with new features. It also required a different strategy to test the final product, because current methods were unable to meet the complexity requirements. I thought this was an exciting project. I knew the technology was challenging, but I did not realize the possible impact of increased risk. The project was progressing very slowly, but the risks became more evident as the project progressed.

How NLP Performs Sentiment Analysis
As we know, project management is filled with words that are unique or at least very common to project management activities. Words such as "scope," "schedule," and "risk" are frequently used by project

managers. Phrases such as "earned value," "schedule delay," and "scope creep" are probably unique to communications in the world of projects. Machine learning includes sentiment analysis capability, which is a method to determine whether specific text should be classified as positive or negative. This can be a valuable tool for a project manager. For example, a project manager may want to validate the effectiveness of a new communication strategy. Or perhaps the project manager simply wants to monitor project communication in order to become proactive and respond quickly to any negative sentiment.

The ethics of monitoring organizational communication is a separate topic that can be debated. For now, the focus will be the capability of AI or machine learning software. Monitoring project communications in an organization uses all communication mechanisms as input. This includes emails, instant messages, and other documents that may be produced. It may also include smartphone conversations, text messages, or any verbal communication that is captured. For this content the focus is on text interpretation.

The first step is to filter all text input to capture the content that relates to the project. This can be accomplished by searching for key words, such as the project name or proper names of project team members and the project sponsor. The code in Python programming language to search for a project name looks like this:

```
# Search the content for the project name in the file Wordlist (all words have been transformed to lower case)
>> re.findall(r 'project name', Wordlist)
```

The content is then processed to remove meaningless words such as "the" and "and." There are utilities that make this easy to perform.

\# Removing words from the content to produce a filtered wordlist
\>> stop_words = set(stopwords.words('english'))
\>> filtered_wordlist = [w for w in tokenized_text if not w in stop_words]

In order to classify the data into positive and negative sentiment, a repository is used based on labeled data. In other words, there is a file of content that contains positive comments and another that contains negative comments. The content in these files is used to compare a new incoming text. However, before this happens it is best to nullify the impact of project management jargon. Therefore, a list is created that contains "neutral" words or phrases. Here is an example:

\# Remove the impact of project management words that are commonly used
\>> neutral_vocab = ['schedule', 'budget', 'project', 'manager', 'results', 'costs']

The software is trained using a machine learning utility, and then test data is supplied to validate the model. The accuracy of the results is dependent on numerous items, and the amount of training data is the largest factor. Once an accurate model is built, it can be a very useful tool for project managers.

Stakeholder Management Using Sentiment Analysis

This type of tool may seem invasive, but it is actually in place now for other purposes. In marketing, consumers are tracked to capture their preferences. Software such as location analytics and facial recognition is used by retailers and mall owners to track and measure customer shopping behavior.[14] The objective is to optimize store performance and ultimately increase profits. Within an organization, employees might be required to provide consent to allow the tracking of their words and activities. However, employees are using the organization's email servers, so it may be considered acceptable to perform email analysis by machine learning tools. It is likely that this type of tool will be used in an organization for general purposes before being used strictly for project management. However, it offers a project manager an enormous advantage from existing methods to communicate with stakeholders and proactively de-escalate problems.

In the future, an AI tool such as this will be constantly scanning employee communication and categorizing sentiment to provide the project manager with clear and timely recommendations about how to address a variety of issues. It is possible that this type of tool will become indispensable to the organization. Will the benefits outweigh the privacy concerns? The next step is obviously to monitor employee actions outside the workplace, which is already in place for social media posts for a number of organizations. This is implemented legally by creating a policy and informing employees. In many cases there is an expected level of professionalism from employees at all times in the public. Think of professional athletes who received discipline for behaving poorly outside their normal place of work. Similarly, a project stakeholder can be monitored while engaged in conversations after normal working hours or perhaps even while not discussing work-related activities. The acceptance of this level of scrutiny will be determined eventually by either employee acceptance or government intervention.

Searching social media for information about a project or stakeholder is fairly simple. It only takes four lines of code to search and find

---

14 Sarah Rieger, "At Least Two Malls Are Using Facial Recognition Technology to Track Shoppers' Ages and Genders Without Telling," CBC News, July 26, 2018, https://www.cbc.ca/news/canada/calgary/calgary-malls-1.4760964.

content related to a stakeholder. Content after the pound symbol is used to explain the code and is ignored by the software program.

Sample code:
name1 = df.iloc[0,0]   # pull stakeholder name from a dataframe
from bs4 import BeautifulSoup # use a utility for data scraping
import urllib2
quote_page = "http://www. " # identify websites and pull website data

Of course, there needs to be verification of identification of either the stakeholder or the project name. The point is to illustrate how simple and feasible it is to grab information from social media to perform further actions such as sentiment analysis.

The organization will need to determine what level of sentiment analysis is required or will be permitted. High-level tracking and summarization of results where the users remain anonymous is less invasive and still provides valuable information such as the trend of positive or negative feelings toward the progress of the project. On the other hand, tracking individuals is far more effective, yet this leads to ethical issues. Individuals may not want to work on a project that uses this type of tracking, and people who are project stakeholders might feel intimidated.

The individual-tracking AI tool is likely to be the most controversial in terms of ethics. Is it acceptable to have an algorithm read and analyze emails and text messages? Perhaps this would be acceptable for an organization that has a very open culture and is determined to have successful project results or a very overbearing organization that wants project success at any cost. The purpose of this discussion is not to judge the ethics or any organization or AI tool but rather to present the capability that is available.

There is also a possibility of having microphones in project meetings to capture conversations. In fact, some project meetings are recoded deliberately in order to retain accurate records of decisions. However, an alternative use would be to capture dialogue and analyze sentiment. That might seem more invasive and have implications for the level of communication that makes an individual feel uncomfortable with contributing. It is not a topic for further analysis in this context. It only reveals the incredible disruption that AI tools will have.

Making the sentiment results anonymous is a more palatable alternative. In other words, the project manager may report a sentiment trend of a grouping of stakeholders without actually knowing the names of the stakeholders. Similarly, the project sponsor can have access to a project sentiment analysis, which illustrates the trend across all stakeholders or within the project team. This can be used proactively to address issues and improve the project culture and relationships.

Improving Project Team Communication

Can machine learning analysis help people by communicating directly with them? Spotify ran an ad campaign on billboards after analyzing listener data. In the UK, 3,749 people streamed the song "It's the End of the World as We Know It" the day after the majority of people voted to withdraw from the European Union. The Spotify billboard reads: "Dear 3,749 people who streamed 'It's the End of the World as We Know It' the day of the Brexit vote, hang in there."[15]

An analysis of project team utterances can result in an output of positive and encouraging words. Spotify found a way to humanize the results in a creative and playful way. That should also be one of the

---

15 Tim Nudd, "Spotify Crunches User Data in Fun Ways for This New Global Outdoor Ad Campaign," Adweek, November 29, 2016, https://www.adweek.com/creativity/spotify-crunches-user-data-fun-ways-new-global-outdoor-ad-campaign-174826/.

goals for NLP tools in project management. One of my team members completed a task in the project task tracking tool Asana, and a unicorn flew by on the screen as a reward. Health monitoring products such as Fitbits and Apple Watches find creative ways to encourage people to take those extra steps and give encouraging messages when goals are achieved. When I teach my students, I try some gamification by letting them earn badges for completing simple tasks such as reading the course outline and the schedule for course content. I also use the quiz tool Kahoot, and the student with the highest score wins a small prize. This is starting to get off track, but the purpose is to illustrate that machine learning and NLP tools can have a positive impact on people by analyzing communication and then responding in an appropriate way.

It is important to analyze the project status in terms of the objectives and emotions of the project team. Based on communication, NLP can assess satisfaction, stress, and frustration as the project progresses and allow an opportunity to respond or give feedback immediately rather than wait for worsening conditions. It enables proactive action rather than reactive. Also, improved communication based on individual personality is more effective than a generic response. For example, introverts need time to process. They prefer to receive prior notification with a clear topic so they are not surprised.

Software tools have the potential to make us comfortable and not fearful or intimidated. On the other hand, they can be invasive and annoying. As a loving father I searched the internet one day and bought a baby gift for my daughter, and now based on the ads that I'm seeing, the internet thinks that I'm the one who is pregnant.

The Future of AI Based Stakeholder Management

Here are two examples of how powerful NLP can be. The first example is about children under the age of eight, who are unable to properly express emotional suffering. Therefore, it is the responsibility of adults to recognize problems and seek treatment. Recently developed AI tools can now detect depression based on a child's speech, and with early diagnosis children respond well to treatment.[16] The second example is from the *New York Times*. A voice analysis software program has been developed that not only understands human speech but also is capable of detecting post-traumatic stress disorder.[17] The algorithm is trained to listen for minor variables and auditory markers that are imperceptible to the human ear. The algorithm can diagnose PTSD with 89 percent accuracy.

Based on a person's voice, AI can detect mental illness and possibly other medical conditions. If a person slurs their speech during a tense project status meeting, are they having a stroke? The potential for sentiment analysis goes significantly beyond positive or negative feelings toward a project. Voice analysis tools will be able to identify when someone is nervous about being able to achieve the end date for a task but does not want to reveal any problems. People who are overly aggressive on goals or claim they can perform more work than they are capable of performing will be evident to an AI tool. While this may seem invasive to a person's privacy, if the goal is to increase success rates on a project, why not implement them? There are so many workshops, courses, and published research documents on how a project manager needs to improve interactions with people, and here we have a tool that will be invaluable. Is there a difference if a well-trained project manager detects a problem in a person's commitments versus a well-trained machine learning tool that identifies the same condition?

Facial recognition is used to identify a person's age, gender, and even emotions at a given moment. Will this be done with project

---

16 University of Vermont. "AI can detect depression in a child's speech." ScienceDaily. www.sciencedaily.com/releases/2019/05/190506150126.htm (accessed September 8, 2019), https://www.sciencedaily.com/releases/2019/05/190506150126.htm.
17 Dave Philipps, "The Military Wants Better Tests for PTSD. Speech Analysis Could Be the Answer," *The New York Times Magazine*, April 19, 2019, https://www.nytimes.com/2019/04/22/magazine/veterans-ptsd-speech-analysis.html.

stakeholders in order to manage them effectively? AI will test the limits of what we are willing to accept in terms of how we manage people on a project. Does the result justify the method? If the method provides a positive benefit not only to the project outcome but also the project manager and project team members, then it may be easier to accept. We wear Apple Watches and Fitbits to track or maintain a healthy regimen. The goal is to transfer that to a project team where a more positive environment is created, and that in turn increases the probability of project success. Who wants to be on a project that is consistently over budget and late?

On the other hand, technology tools can be used for purposes other than what they were designed for, and that can easily happen in this situation. Project managers may try to find a way to replace team members who are too nervous and not forthcoming or try to mold a team into a group of people who are driven to succeed. The same tool that has the ability to create a positive and sharing project team environment has the ability to do the opposite depending on how the data is used. Privacy will still be an issue if the organization cannot maintain confidentiality of personal information. A person might be having a bad day and not be particularly friendly, and that information should not be made available to other people, organizations, or social media. Who can predict what the implementation of a sentiment analysis tool will look like and how the organization will manage and control the results? Regardless, this is a powerful AI tool, and hopefully project teams will find a way to achieve the benefits while avoiding all the pitfalls.

Story: Personal Bias
People have a natural bias that can be harsher than a machine learning bias. I worked for an up-and-coming software firm that saw significant growth. There were several project managers in the professional services organization. I met a woman who worked in administration and

seemed very nice. My personal interactions with her were limited, although she was always friendly and treated me with respect. I responded by doing the same. One of my coworkers, however, was not as kind. He may have heard that she received a poor performance review or that she was not as educated as he was. When she worked with him, I would overhear a condescending attitude in the next cubicle. Somehow, he developed a personal internal bias against this woman that was not related to their commitment to complete the tasks required. I never understood that and continued to maintain a friendly relationship with the woman after she left the organization and moved to a new position in a different company. Machine learning tools can develop a bias when all they learn from is historical information. People can also develop a bias toward someone, and they are less likely to find a way to eliminate that bias than the bias in a machine learning algorithm.

Summary
Managing stakeholders is one of the more challenging tasks for a project manager. An AI tool can be a powerful assistant to help with this responsibility. The process is complex, requiring the ability to understand project management vocabulary as well as to identify different stakeholder personalities. The result is an output that has the capability to optimize personal interactions on the project. Using NLP-based analysis on people can be invasive, but it can also be rewarding and motivating. There need to be creative solutions including privacy and ethical consideration in order to be successful. Overall it still offers an opportunity to vastly improve team member and all stakeholder communications.

VIRTUAL ASSISTANTS

If you have an iPhone, you know about Siri. If your computer uses a Microsoft operating system, you may have seen Cortana. These voice-enabled tools act as assistants to the user in order to find information or complete tasks. Also known as chatbots or virtual personal assistants, they are frequently found in a messaging format on websites to interact with customers searching for information. The AI part is able to recognize and interpret sequences of words and give them meaning in a way that a response can be created. I have Amazon's Alexa at home and ask for weather updates or to play music for dinner. Alexa is also very good at settling disagreements that you may have with a spouse, relative, or friend, because in response to a question, she can check a reliable internet source and tell you the correct answer.

While a voice recognition system that can play your favorite music on command seems low value, this tool is gaining momentum in the business world. This is equivalent to handsfree on your smartphone but involves talking to a database. There is a business that will let you load all your organization's documents and then allow them to be queried by a voice enabled chatbot. This is a great opportunity for project managers to load a scope document, for example, and allow team members the option of reading or making verbal queries to get data instantly. The next step is to find a way to load the current project status, including an update strategy, which can be either a batch style update on a predetermined schedule or a streaming update in real time. Following this, the final piece to the puzzle is a source document that can apply project management logic to the data.

Imagine all of your project management plan documents loaded to a voice-enabled agent that contains project management logical connections and interpretation. You ask if a specific task that is due this week can be moved to the following week. The agent replies that yes, this is possible because the task is not on the critical path, but it adds that a risk is attached to the task, and it will increase the risk probability from 20 percent to 30 percent. The agent identified that the task was not on the critical path and then identified that it was linked to a risk in the risk register. Finally, it gave the project manager an update on the risk changes. Now the project manager can investigate further or make a decision whether to move the task to the following week. This is a very simple example of what is possible. It also illustrates the concept that I call ubiquitous project management. That means you can manage a project from anywhere at any time as long as you have access to your agent, and this is normally done using a smartphone.

One of my favorite things about Alexa is her honesty. When I ask Alexa to play the greatest hits from a band that I loved when I was growing up, Alexa plays one song, then stops. I guess they were not as popular as I remembered.

Historical Data

The data required to build a virtual assistant consists of several documents. The project management planning documents are used to reply to queries and remain as static documents unless changed by an approved change order, which needs to be captured and updated in the database. During project execution additional documents may be added in order to track the progress of the project in more detail. In addition, updates are made to the original project documents, such as the project schedule, resource calendar, resource availability, risk register, stakeholder register, and communication plan. Once these are captured and updated in a timely manner, the documents can also be queried regarding the current project status.

Similar to the stakeholder management AI tool, a project management corpus is required to understand the specific language used for managing projects. If practical, this may be used in common with the stakeholder management tool that also uses NLP to evaluate sentiment.

The most complex and intriguing document will be the one that provides the logic behind complex queries that ask specific project management questions such as if a task is on the critical path or what is the best method to manage a risk that has caused a task to be delayed. PMBOK is one source of logic, although there are many opportunities, and developers may not be inclined to use a copyright resource that is subject to changes on a regular basis. It has important content but may be considered unmanageable since it is out of the control of both the organizations and project stakeholders. Also, projects exist in rapidly changing environments, and a logic source needs to reflect the most recent best practices.

More About NLP

Natural language processing is a technique that treats words as data and performs analysis on the data to understand it. Python programming language has a natural language tool kit (NLTK) that contains helpful processing functions, and it also applies statistics to the words so they can be analyzed and used in prediction and classification.

As mentioned previously, the process incudes several steps such as removing words that don't add value, such as "the," "a," and "in." NLP identifies words as the correct parts of speech including nouns, verbs, adjectives, pronouns, and adverbs, which is important in order to understand their meaning. It can assess single words or any series of words, such as a phrase. The capability also includes the ability to identify named entities, which include person names, organizations, locations, time expressions, and quantities. This helps with the meaning of text but also can be used to match the entity used in a verbal expression to an entity in a document or detect the project name in an email.

The terminology for building a chatbot includes the following items. An *utterance* is anything that someone says and is taken as a verbal input to the chatbot. An *intent* is what the person wants to know.

Based on the utterance and similar utterances, the model determines what it is that the user is asking. An *entity* can be part of an intent and identifies a characteristic that can have alternatives, such as "today," or "yesterday," or can identify a person's name that is contained in the utterance. A default response is added so that there is always a response. As indicated above it might be, "Sorry, I seem to be busy right now. Try again later," or something more specific to project management might be, "I don't think you really want to know that."

A common method in text classification is called Naive Bayes. It is based on Bayes' theorem, which is used in statistics to predict the probability of an event based on a certain condition. In Naive Bayes classifiers, the events are considered independent (i.e., naive) of each other. This type of classifier is commonly used to categorize text or text documents as belonging to one group or another. While the equation can be difficult to understand, the coding is easy in Python and can be done by importing the module that you want to use. The purpose of using classification is to identify queries that have the same intent or meaning, such as the ones listed below.

> What is my next task?
> Give me my next tasks.
> What task should I work on next?
> What activity should I work on next?

These queries are asking the same thing, and the AI tool identifies and responds to all of them with the same response, which is the next project task that is assigned to this resource.

At the heart of the tool is the *response framework*, which is developed to match the intent to the appropriate content in a database. This is where logic is required to select and compose the response. The chatbot needs to be trained to recognize the various utterances that mean the same intent, and as always there must be a feedback loop that provides constant improvement and updates.

The process for communicating with a virtual assistant starts with an utterance.

Example 1
Utterance: Is there training in the scope document?

The tool needs to discover the intent. This means it needs to look for a relationship to the content. For this utterance, it needs to find training information. "Training" is a noun. It searches the project document repository for the scope document, and within the scope document, it searches for the training section. Once the training section is found, it reads the words and replies by converting the words to a verbal response.

Example 2
A project team member sends an email to a coworker.

Utterance (written): I am not happy with my assignment. I don't have enough experience to complete these tasks on time.

NLP performs sentiment analysis. The phrase "not happy" is a negative expression. This is categorized as a negative sentiment and is included in the general project sentiment trend indicator or highlighted for the project manager, who can make a decision about what actions to take to monitor or remediate the situation.

Building a Virtual Assistant for Project Management
A typical data flow for a virtual assistant tool is shown in figure 3.5.

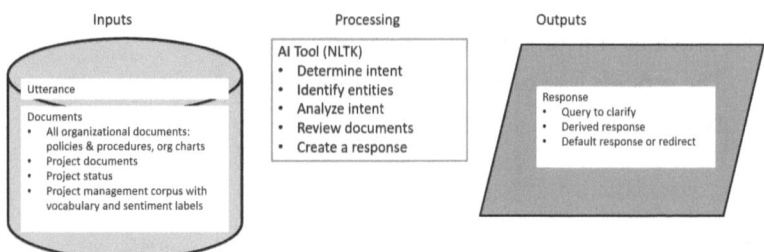

Figure 3.5

Inputs. An utterance is what we say or type, and NLP has the ability to interpret variations to mean the same request. I can say, "Give me the status report," "I want the status report," or, "What is the latest status?" and receive an update on the status of the project. NLP performs classification to match these utterances as meaning the same thing. An utterance can be verbal or text communication.

The organization documents are available to the agent, such as policies and procedures and the organization chart, which identifies roles and responsibilities of employees in the organization as well as the project team. This means that the agent can receive a query and respond based on organizational documents. Project management documents can be loaded with the project plans. This takes the queries to another level, because now project information can be accessed by the project manager or team members from an agent on a smartphone. The next step is to update the project documents to reflect the current project status. This can be challenging as to whether live streaming data is allowed or a physical update to project documents such as the project schedule is necessary. Live streaming data would include hourly activity as the team members work. The problem with live data is volatility that does not represent actual progress. Think of a statistical distribution where the initial reported data is far from the mean in one direction. Once all the data is recorded, there is a normal distribution, but in the moment, it may seem to be skewed in one direction or the other, which leads to a misleading conclusion. That is something a project manager needs to avoid. In order to interpret the utterances properly, a project management vocabulary is needed, and this is typically provided in the form of a corpus for project management language. This reduces misinterpretation of language, since project management terms can often have a unique or specific meaning.

Processing. For voice communication the agent classifies the utterances as an intent. If the intent is not understood or does not exist, the agent will ask for clarification. Once the intent is understood, the agent may search a document and issue a response. For complex queries involving project management concepts, the agent needs to understand the entire project and access the logic database to formulate the best response based on machine learning output. Not only is the logic important, but it can also include project metrics such as earned value or resource-leveling issues. The ultimate goal is to elevate the concept of ubiquitous project management to allow access not only to project data but also logic that can determine the best response and allow a virtual assistant to make a recommendation based on a holistic perspective of the project. As with other AI tools, there is a need to provide updates to the model so that it remains current.

Outputs. The output in its simplest form is the reply to a query from a static document. If the query is not understood, the virtual assistant can ask questions to seek clarification in order to classify the query properly. However, if a logic source is applied, then there will be even more evaluation as well as invoking of a different machine learning algorithm to determine the best solution to a complex query involving project management concepts. A simple query regarding a task on the critical path may require analysis of other factors such as resources, risks, quality, and stakeholder thresholds. This is the only way to ensure that the response includes the total project interdependences. As a last resort for queries that cannot be properly answered, the agent can redirect the question to another source, such as a live person or a series of documents.

The Personal Assistant

A flash briefing is a skill that can be set up in Alexa or other agents and is similar to a podcast or short status update on any topic desired. It could typically be a brief report on the financial markets followed by local news. It can also be created to provide updates on a variety of content, such as current exchange rates, status of the housing market, or the latest sports results. This can be used in project management to create an audio status report based on project content and results. For a project manager, this can be set up to provide a project overview and include any metrics produced by the project reports. It can also focus on a specific topic, such as a list and status of the current issues on the project and the results to date on achieving a resolution.

The project team needs to be very vigilant in creating structured documents so that NLP can read and interpret them properly. There may be some missteps along the way, such as when you ask the agent to tell you the project status in front a room of project stakeholders, and it responds with an obscure comment like, "This project is definitely not feeling well today," or my favorite phrase from Alexa, "Sorry, I seem to be busy right now; please try again later." This is referred to by some people as the fun side of new technology.

A more complicated skill will be to add logic to the project management content to provide decision support to the project manager. What tasks are on the critical path? What risks are no longer a concern for the project because they have moved to a zero probability? The assistant needs to access a logic source that will interpret the project management concepts and apply them to the content from the project documents.

It is also important to create a holistic solution, which imposes another layer of intelligence to the logic. You do not want a response that says it is acceptable to delay a task that was not on the critical path only to find out later that moving it created a significant negative impact on quality.

Embrace the change! A virtual assistant is available twenty-four hours a day, seven days a week, which is ideal for remote workers as well as a globally dispersed team. It may also benefit an insomniac project manager. Agents give an instant response and translate information into different languages. All of this is great news as long as we learn how to properly work with them. Until the agent is fully trained and understands project management vocabulary, it will be important to phrase certain questions correctly in order to receive a response that accurately interprets results such as project spending and the project schedule. It will be important to be precise, for example, by indicating a specific date or time frame for a data summary. There may also be nuances of language that do not translate as easily, especially with project management jargon.

A project management chatbot or virtual assistant needs access to utterances and should determine intents that are specific to the language of project management. Also, chatbots are either stateless or stateful. A stateless agent assumes that the conversation is with a new person, and no prior history is considered. A stateful agent understands that this is a person who had a previous conversation, and that experience can be used to provide better responses and understand the utterances better. The trend is to make functions easier, and an intelligent virtual assistant has that capability. The agent could be a custom solution for an organization, or in the future there might be skill sets that can be added to existing agents such as Alexa, Siri, or Google Assistant.

One final word on communicating directly with a virtual assistant is that NLP is confused by sarcasm, which is difficult to assess and can be more complex to decipher. Humans say funny things sometimes.

In order to manage the tool properly, there may need to be a hierarchy of permissions. An example is in table 10.

Table 10: Sample Project Document Access Permissions

Role/output	Project plans	Current project status	Machine learning recommendations
Project manager	Read/update	Available	Access
Project team	Read/section updates	Available	Limited access
General stakeholders	Read only	Limited availability to key activities	No access

The Future of Virtual Assistants for Project Management

The concept of ubiquitous project management can help the entire project team improve communications. Imagine a global team of over one hundred people being able to access the project information. As documents are updated, such as a change request log or a risk register, everyone will have access to the same information. There will be an ability to receive important project updates similar to the way we set our notification settings on a website such as LinkedIn or one of those sales sites such as Wayfair. Of course, if you are getting inundated with communication, remember that you are the one who set it up that way. When that project change request is approved, the project manager will know immediately. The communication can be direct voice, voice message, text message, or email.

There will also be flawless logic behind the documents that supports decision-making ability as the virtual assistance is combined with an intelligent agent that can search through documents to gain knowledge, gather data from sensors, and perform data mining. What is the best task to reschedule in order to free up a specific resource? The tool can respond with the best answer after reviewing all the options based on sound project management logic. Not only is there a response, but it will be the best recommendation for the situation. For decision-making, a tool such as the predictor tool can be integrated so the project manager can assess the success prediction of alternative decisions. Please choose the one that results in a higher probability of success.

The project can be managed from anywhere at any time, as long as you have access to your virtual assistant. It will also allow you to manage multiple projects at the same time. Simply invoke the project name for the latest updates. This is a great tool for a PMO, as long as the culture is one of openness and positive support. AI tools should be productive and promote confidence within the project team and project stakeholders. Achieving a high project success rate will solidify the tool as reliable and indispensable.

A virtual assistant allows the use of ubiquitous project management, which is the ability to manage a project from anywhere at any time. For a project manager, it means the ability to access project data easily and instantly and make decisions based on input from a machine learning algorithm. For project stakeholders it can mean accessing project information without searching documents or having to communicate directly with the project team. This provides less distraction for the project team. The project team can also access the documents but may provide input or opinions that are collected and sent to the project manager. Messages can be tagged to a specific task, project issue, or project document.

In the future an added feature for chatbots when accessed using a smartphone is to have facial recognition capability that identifies the person accessing the project. In addition, the capability can be enhanced with other AI tools such as the predictor tool, expert systems, and simulation software to turn this into a truly intelligent virtual assistant.

RESOLVING ISSUES SUCCESSFULLY

Projects are very complex, and regardless of our careful planning, problems always arise as the project is executed. It would be ideal to have a machine learning tool that could predict issues during the planning phase of the project and allow us to include them in the risk register with a proper mitigation plan. Regardless, there will still be issues that need to be resolved, from smaller problems such as an absent team member to larger problems such as the client having a conflicting interpretation of the scope statement. Having a machine learning tool that supports good decisions when issues arise is an ideal use for AI technology.

The Issues Log

Projects normally have a regular status meeting internally with the project team, externally with clients, or both. During this meeting or even outside of the meeting, issues or problems arise and are captured in a report known as the issues log. As project managers know, nothing ever goes perfectly on a project. Developing a machine learning tool to manage issues and problems consists of two opportunities. The first is to train a machine learning algorithm based on previous projects to predict issues for a newly proposed project. What is the likelihood of encountering a specific schedule delay, for example? At least when you know this beforehand, the item can be added to the risk register, and a mitigation plan can be created. The ultimate goal is to know all possible problems before the project begins. After all, project managers do not like surprises, especially negative ones, and especially in the middle of project execution.

The second opportunity for a machine learning tool is to recommend the best solution for any issue that occurs during the project. In spite of all the planning, unpredictable problems will inevitably happen. A machine learning tool can use historical data to find the best solution given the nature of the project and how similar issues were resolved.

The input documents are critical and include the lessons learned from previous projects and the issues log from previous projects with the outcome of the action taken to resolve the issue labeled as successful or not. The project documents are also important, as they define the project strategy and are used as input to train the model before the project begins.

Historical Data

Having sufficient historical data will always be important. It is also important that the documents are formatted properly and contain the proper categorization of the data. For example, in the issues log, the actions taken to resolve issues need to be saved and labeled as successful or not. In my experience the lessons learned document can take many forms and is normally created with the objective of improving the project processes so that the issue is prevented from ever happening again. That does not always work. Most resolutions identified in a lessons learned document result in either procedure updates or ways to improve communication. This outcome can make the training for a machine learning tool more complicated. The objective is to train the algorithm to recognize and predict similar problems in future projects. That might be accomplished by evaluating whether the actions taken after a lessons learned issue have been implemented in the organization's policies. In addition, many projects do not document a formal lessons learned when the project has gone well. Therefore, there is often very little or no training data available for successful projects. We can think of a project as if it were a lung x-ray image, where the machine learning algorithm has been trained to verify or dismiss a potential problem. This concept of the project as an image can be useful in order to understand how a machine learning tool determines a classification.

Table 11: Using an Issues Log AI Tool

Stage	Opportunity
Prior to the project	Classify historical issues with a probability to occur on the proposed project
During the project	Predict the most successful solutions
After the project	Use issue resolution results to train the machine learning tools in a reinforcement learning process

Building an AI Issues Tool for Project Management
A typical data flow for an issues tool is shown in figure 3.6.

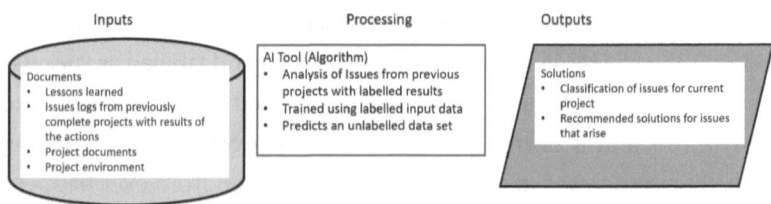

Figure 3.6

Inputs. The process uses several documents as input to the algorithm as indicated in the diagram. Lessons learned documents will be critical in this process, as they can be expected to contain many areas where the project failed to plan for the issues either as a risk or in the plans themselves. Similarly, the issues log will contain unexpected problems that previous projects have encountered. The project environment data provides additional input and can be used by a machine learning tool to correlate similar circumstances as well as similar outcomes.

Processing. Processing includes an analysis of the data, and training occurs so that the machine learning tool can predict or classify new issues. The first part of training is to identify possible issues from historical projects that have not been captured in the plans for the new project. The next training goal is to identify actions that provide the best solution for any issues that arise during project execution. Finally, it will be important to use the results of the issue resolutions as further input to the machine learning tools as part of ensuring that the data is up to date.

Outputs. As mentioned, the two basic outputs are the identification of issues not included in project plans and the recommended solutions for new issues that arise during the project execution stage.

The Future of an Issues Log Tool

In an ideal project setting, a machine learning tool will be able to predict problems in advance and allow the project manager to take proactive measures to prevent or quickly resolve them. In the event that an issue arises at the last moment, the machine learning tool can recommend an optimum solution based on what has worked in the past and the current project status, organization, and external environment. Both of these outcomes increase the probability of project success. Eventually this type of tool will be indispensable and can be connected to the project database for constant updates to the data which will improve the tool's accuracy.

Story: Issues Report
I once worked on a very complex project with a difficult and demanding client. The weekly status meetings were often tense, and any issues reported were immediately captured and either resolved at the time or listed in the issues and actions report. My boss was the meeting chairperson and was also responsible for recording and issuing the meeting's action items that required people to follow up and either report back at the next meeting or implement a solution by a given date. My boss was also a meticulous person who always looked for efficiencies. The column headings on the report included the issue number, description, due date, and other categories. There was one column used to identify the action to be taken, and it was listed as "follow up" where the problem was not yet resolved. The column next to it indicated the person assigned to resolve the issue. Trying to be efficient and reduce words, my boss combined these into one column with no heading, but beside every unresolved issue were the words "follow up" and the name of the person responsible. The following week he abbreviated the words "follow up" using the first letter of each word, then added the person's name beside it, which resulted in something like this: "FU: George, FU: Ahmed." I tell this anecdote in class and get blank stares from my international students who do not have a full grasp on the English language. Then I tell them that the term "F you" is vulgar slang in English. It will be important for an AI tool to have and use proper English and hopefully never make a similar mistake.

AN AI CHANGE CONTROL TOOL

One of the great values of artificial intelligence technology is the ability to access vast amounts of data, perform analysis, evaluate alternatives, and make decisions. For project management this is a significant opportunity. Consider the implications for a change request where a new requirement is proposed, and the project manager and project team consider the impact of the change on both the budget and schedule. They collect data and respond with the potential increase in cost and delay in schedule. In reality, the change might affect numerous additional areas of the project, which can create unexpected negative consequences. In a situation of several change requests at the same time, the complexity of interdependences may be too difficult to analyze for an accurate evaluation. An AI tool can manage both complexity and vast amounts of data and can produce a more accurate assessment of the impact of the changes on the project.

Historical Data
Having properly formatted data should be easier with change control data, because most organizations have good standards and common templates for integrated change control. There are two parts to this. The first is a change request log that captures all requested changes and whether they are approved. The second is the actual change document itself, which typically provides an abundance of detailed data that can be used by machine learning tools.

The lessons learned document from previous projects is also important, because it may contain potential changes that previous projects did not anticipate. This can result in a machine learning tool classifying lessons learned issues or predicting them as potential changes to the current project.

Managing Changes
An AI tool is ideal for managing change in a project. Remember the two characteristics of machine learning? Prediction and classification. Based on the project scope for a similar project and comparing it thoroughly to the scope of a new project, an AI tool should be able to predict scope changes that will be requested. Next, based on a change

request to the existing scope, a machine learning tool should be able to classify the change in terms of being successfully implemented and make a prediction of the impact on the project in terms of schedule and budget as well as the other knowledge areas. AI needs to be a holistic solution, and this is a good example where all aspects of the project need to be considered.

Table 12: Using a Project AI Change Control Tool

Stage	Activity	AI change control tool usage
Project planning	Create a complete scope statement	Predict potential changes to the project scope statement
Changes requested during project execution	Assess the implications and implement approved changes	Verify the impact and identify the best method for successful implementation

Change requests are not limited to scope and can be process changes required for the project methodology as part of corrective or preventive action. Changes can be made to project documents or policies and procedures used to manage the project. A significant concern is when proposed changes have an impact on any project baseline, such as cost, schedule, quality, or risk. AI tools may be used to identify alternative ways to implement these changes and try to minimize or eliminate any negative repercussions. A cost-benefit analysis of a proposed change can be done by other IT tools, but a machine learning tool can predict whether the analysis is within certain limits. It will also be important that the analysis includes all interdependent relationships, since the change may create an unintended negative side effect either within the project or with other projects in the organization. AI tools need to have a holistic perspective of the project, since that is a responsibility that is also expected of a project manager.

Building an AI Tool for Change Control

A typical data flow for a change control tool is shown in figure 3.7. This is similar to the issues data flow, and it is possible that the same machine learning algorithm could be used for both situations. The difference is in the input data provided for each objective.

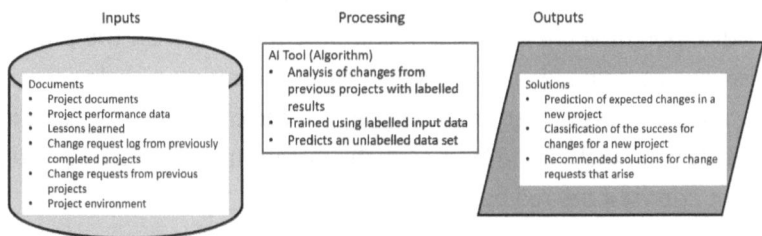

Figure 3.7

Inputs. The inputs are similar to those in the issues tool, but this tool includes historical data for both the change request log with the results of the change being approved or not and the change request itself with all the data fields. Once the algorithm is trained, the data for a newly proposed project is analyzed. All relevant sections of the project documents are used as input, since this aligns with the holistic approach required by project managers. Perhaps the change request will have an unexpected impact on a risk. The project status is used as a basis for understanding the impact. Lessons learned documents will be important, because problems from previous projects might indicate a change is required to the current project.

Change requests are normally well organized and implemented in a controlled manner in most organizations. There is an opportunity to increase the amount of valuable data captured in each change request document, including the method used to implement the change and an evaluation of the success of the implementation. The machine learning algorithm needs access to all the appropriate data to produce accurate results. Therefore, the change request form may need to be updated to include additional content.

Processing. The processing includes training an algorithm to recognize a scope statement that subsequently had to be adjusted in order to achieve the project objective. The machine learning tool can then predict potential changes that will impose a new risk on the project. Also, the machine learning tool will use classification to help identify the most successful method to implement the changes. This might include factors such as the least cost, the fastest implementation, or different criteria if desired by the organization.

Outputs. Ideally, a machine learning tool makes a prediction of probable changes before they are requested. This prediction is based on similar previous projects as well as the project status. The tool should also predict the probability of success of the change based on having a positive or negative impact on the project baseline. In addition, where an implementation path is uncertain, the machine learning tool can recommend the optimal solution for making the change while minimizing the impact.

The Future of a Change Control Tool

A predictive analytics algorithm can be used to identify the impact of a change on all aspects of the project. Change requests normally highlight the impact on cost and schedule and then reduce or ignore the impact on risk, quality, resources, and other aspects of the project. A fully functioning AI tool for change control should be able to predict changes at the start of the project, which allows them to be added to the risk register. During the project, new changes can be evaluated with a machine learning algorithm to determine the probability of the change being successfully implemented. It would be nice if there were no changes on a project, but that is unlikely. Change in the environment is constant, and therefore, changes in the project plans should always be expected. If a project is subject to a constant and significant number of unexpected changes, the project methodology probably needs to change to accommodate this situation. AI tools can be used to predict or classify expected changes that will result in a more realistic scope statement that can be delivered on time and within the budget.

ADDITIONAL AI TOOLS AND RESOURCES

Agile methodology typically has a daily stand-up meeting that promotes communication, collaboration, and a focus on completing immediate activities. It is an environment that is more accepting of change and finds ways to adapt to it. There is also an increased focus on quality by identifying and resolving issues earlier in the project. Since agile is based on an iterative approach during the execution stage of the project, the concept of data streaming to a machine learning algorithm might be the basis for AI tools. For managing user stories, which comprise a narrative of the scope for an iteration, a tool such as ScopeMaster can be effective. ScopeMaster is a fascinating tool that combines AI with existing project management concepts. It was developed by Colin Hammond in the United Kingdom and uses NLP to analyze the scope statement or agile user stories to measure functional size based on the cost estimating technique known as function point analysis. This results in the discovery of errors or inconsistencies. It is used for software development and enhancement projects and is especially valuable because finding and correcting errors at this early stage of the project is huge. We know in software projects that finding errors or omissions during a late stage, such as user acceptance test, can lead to increased cost and significant delays in the project. Finding them at the early stages is a tremendous benefit.

The tool uses NLP as well as other modules to analyze written documents. It is web hosted and uses subscriber-based costing, although it could easily be adapted for on-premise software application for organizations that have that requirement. In addition, this software requirements analysis tool uses the concept of function points to automatically perform automated size estimating based on the requirements. An added benefit to organizations is that finding potential bugs and performing sizing estimates can be an educational tool that helps people learn how to create accurate scope definitions.

In addition to the concepts and tools described, numerous vendors provide software based on AI concepts. The list below is not an endorsement of any of these tools, only a review of how AI tools can creep into the business processes, possibly with success.

Aptage predicts outcomes in terms of risk and probability in estimates for cost and time for software projects using the agile methodology.

Clarizen provides project management and collaboration software. It claims to simplify and automate resource and project management. The software learns from project history and creates a regression model to provide future estimates of budget and task duration.

Lili.ai automates recurring tasks, strives to identify risks, and suggests measures to minimize them. It also helps prioritize to-do lists to reduce wait time.

In addition, there are numerous productivity tools that are not used exclusively for project management such as ClickUp, Rescoper, and ZiveBox. These tools use predictive analytics to forecast task durations or the most efficient resources for a task or offer different information with an alert to keep the activities on schedule.

Resources to Create an AI Tool for Project Management
Once an idea is discovered for how to use AI for project management, you need to create the tool. Below are some interesting resources that can help you understand or even provide help creating the software algorithm.

Fiverr
This is a freelance services site that allows anyone to create a scope statement for the service they want and have qualified bidders try to win the contract. For example, it can be used to create machine learning programs or NLP applications. The rates are very competitive.
www.fiverr.com

Gigster
This site offers coding services especially for entrepreneurs or start-ups, and they have AI expertise. This is typically a higher priced option than Fiverr, and their focus includes enterprise software solutions.
www.gigster.com

Kaggle
The Kaggle website is home to a community of data scientists who share ideas and results from contests in fields such as machine learning. Think of it as Uber for data scientists who earn extra money or learn more by participating, all in their spare time. The competitions are real and can be life changing, such as the machine learning competition to

detect pneumothorax disease based on chest x-ray images. The outcome of the competition for a $30,000 prize is to use an AI tool to triage real images for priority attention and to increase the confidence in the correct diagnosis. A good machine learning algorithm can perform better than technicians in analyzing these tricky images. The site is owned by Google and also offers free courses in machine learning topics such as Python programming and Data visualization.
https://kaggle.com

GitHub
GitHub is an open-source repository where programmers can store and access software code in a controlled manner. It offers good version control, and users can access their section with a unique URL. It is frequently used as a reference source for online programming courses or books that refer to lines of code that can be accessed for practice, which is how I first came across it. It handles both private and public projects.
https://github.com

Stack Overflow
Stack Overflow is a website for software developers to ask questions and get answers from other programmers. It is an open community and offers both private and public forums for solving coding problems. In addition, it allows users to browse through a job listing section.
https://stackoverflow.com

A Neural Network Playground
This is a Google sponsored website that allows users to build and play with a simple neural network used for classification. Once you

understand all the components and make your selections, this gives you a real-time visual display of how the neural network works to classify the data.
https://playground.tensorflow.org

SUMMARY

Project management is a business segment that has been neglected in terms of technology development. Microsoft Project gave us a complex but useful scheduling tool, and now a large variety of other scheduling tools are available. Other tools, such as those that check documents for content or verify consistency in a project plan, were developed as general business tools and adopted by project managers. Agile tools were developed specifically for those types of projects. Given the importance and scale of projects being implemented around the world, it is surprising that project management is still so manual. People want to have a successful project but are not sure what the most effective methodology is to deliver a successful project. It will be interesting to see whether a single set of tools can increase project success rates or whether tools will be customized for specific project types or industries. It will also be interesting to see whether large software companies such as Google or Microsoft jump into the business of creating AI tools for project management. With the gig economy, it is much easier for small businesses to create software tools. Perhaps the vendors for scheduling tools will attempt to alter their tools to include machine learning algorithms. However, for a large project-based organization, there needs to be more change in order to be successful.

The application of AI capability will only be limited by our imaginations. Managing a project is a complex activity with numerous moving parts. There are undoubtedly aspects to performing these activities where AI tools can make a major contribution, and yet it is important to consider all the possibilities. Is there a tradeoff between tools that make tasks more efficient and tools that take a higher-level perspective? We need to think differently and not assume that AI will only be able to make each process or task more efficient. A proliferation of tools for project management is inevitable, and decisions will be required as to the best approach for an organization in acquiring tools to insert into their processes. A suggested strategy for AI tool implementation is discussed in chapter 5.

CHAPTER 4
The Project Methodology

Artificial Intelligence will deliver profound changes to project management in ways that will challenge what you think is possible.

In order to radically change a process, it is important to understand it. Machine learning tools can be used throughout the project processes. This section is not meant to be a forecast of which AI tools will be used to achieve an improvement to project processes. Instead, it discusses project management activities that need to be completed throughout the processes. Can these activities be replaced by AI tools? How will a machine learning tool acquire the data needed to perform the prediction and classification activities that result in better decisions and ultimately improve project success rates? This section may also interest entrepreneurs who are searching for creative ideas that can improve project management processes. The challenge is to think of AI tools that can be deployed as part of each process or ones that will disrupt the overall process. These are the tools that organizations value the most and will want to implement.

PROJECT INITIATION

The project initiation stage is where the concept of making a change begins, and that change requires a project to be created. The business case or value statement is created and contains either financial or strategic benefits, hopefully in quantifiable terms. The value statement is always based on data whether you realize it or not: business growth, market share, new regulations, or other factors that can be quantified. For a nonprofit organization, it can be based on strategic values, which can also be quantified. This might be the value of implementing software to allow members to perform online self-service activities, for example. The value statement gets more difficult when the objective is to land a spaceship on Mars, but even that has a clear cost.

The values used for all of these business cases are based both on data that is internal to the organization, such as cost of resources, desired growth, and increased product margins, and external factors, such as contractor pricing, resource availability, industry or government regulations, and market growth rates. Data is what drives machine learning, and the data is available for all factors, given that enough time is spent acquiring the numbers. In fact, a machine learning tool can generate results from similar projects, assuming there is sufficient data to validate the outcomes when compared to other projects.

This stage also has a project screening or selection process where projects are either screened in for further consideration based on designated criteria or selected based on having the best values compared to other projects. The criteria might be financial, such as payback period or return on investment (ROI), which are very easy to calculate given the proper data.

The opportunities for machine learning include predicting or classifying the correct values to use for the business case, and as the project is implemented, tracking the prediction of whether the values are still valid. I also call this the project euphoria stage. The project is approved, and everyone is happy and excited. For many organizations, it might also be the only time the project is on schedule and under budget, so it is only appropriate to feel good that the project is approved.

PROJECT PLANNING

The first step in planning is to ensure that there is a good scope statement, unless this has been completed in the project charter from the initiation stage. The work breakdown structure (WBS) is transformed into a project schedule with dependencies, durations, and resources. There are various tools that perform schedule verification, which is of great value, but unless they have a way to "learn" from the data, it is not true machine learning or AI.

Budgeting and cost estimating are two ideal areas for AI, where data from the environment or from other similar projects can be applied in order to develop a more accurate budget. Similarly, contingency amounts can be acquired from a machine learning tool that classifies similar projects with similar events and predicts an accurate amount.

Resource assignments can be difficult and are normally based on the task requirements, the skill set of an employee or contractor, and politics. I'm not sure how well AI can help with that third element. Tools exist that use analytics to match assignments to skills, although they may only offer a "good" match and suggest further skills training in order for the work to be completed properly.

Data should be available to help create a risk register and mitigating actions. Similarly, a quality management plan can be based on previously successful project outcomes, although this may be based more on simple statistics than true machine learning with classification.

Quality in project management has two meanings for me. The first and most obvious is whether the final product or service achieves a quality level that is equal to or higher than the quality expected. This can include measurements taken as the project progresses in order to verify the internal quality, which may not be as visible, and the external measurements of the final product or service. An AI tool may be able to review the quality plan of historical projects and predict issues for a new project. Alternately, there may be an ability to discover anomalies that have a potential negative impact on a project.

The second aspect of quality, which may be less obvious, is whether the project itself, such as the project processes or methodology, is being managed to a quality standard that should be expected of successful projects. This can include the effectiveness of communication, timeliness and accuracy of status reports, and timely responses to newly reported problems that arise during the project. It can also include the creation of a good business case as well as accurate and comprehensive project plans during the planning stage. As suggested before, the project methodology needs to use AI tools to achieve higher project success. They also need to be implemented to improve the quality and consistency of the project processes.

Procurement becomes more complicated for small and medium size projects, since there is now a wider array of opportunities for procuring resources. It depends on the type of project and location of work, but sites like Kaggle and Fiverr have turned certain types of procurement into something reminiscent of an eBay auction. This evolution will continue. For large projects, procurement typically includes either the creation of a request for proposal (RFP) or a proposal response, and both of these are good candidates for NLP analysis. NLP analysis can identify errors, omissions, or weaknesses in the documents. Depending on the objective, NLP may also take far less time to analyze a document than human resources assigned to the task. A machine learning tool can assess the external environment and evaluate the optimal fit for a supplier, for example.

PROJECT EXECUTION

This process is where all the work gets done, and it also generates the most real-time data. The work consists of resources being applied to tasks over time. Of course, additional information such as quality results and risk events may also be outcomes of this stage. Changes may be requested and approved. Problems and issues are identified. Procurement contracts can be produced, approved, and performed. Status reports on all this data are created and shared through an appropriate communication method. This is where the action happens, and if the planning is inadequate, incomplete, or simply poor, the executing process is a mess, or as I like to call it, "exciting." However, I can only take so much excitement. The methods may be different depending on whether the approach is waterfall, agile, or a combination of both. Nonetheless, this stage generates the most data and the most variances from the plan. It can be an ideal area for machine learning tools to access and utilize the constantly updated data to keep a project on track.

As a project progresses, it is unusual for everything to go as planned. A lot of tasks are completed, and then some bad things happen. Predictive analytics can be used to help a project schedule understand and manage resources to achieve the time and budget constraints. Data can also be misleading if not used carefully. For example, one task might be budgeted at forty hours and take thirty-two hours to complete. Does that mean all future tasks will only take thirty-two hours? Of course not. Let's say the next forty-hour task actually requires forty-six hours of work. It is this volatility and low sample size that makes predictive analytics difficult. A machine learning tool might be a better solution if it has access to data from numerous similar projects and activities.

This stage is where most, if not all, of the scope changes occur. Whether it is incomplete or ambiguous detail in the original project scope, changes seem inevitable. An AI tool should be able to minimize the changes during the planning process through comparisons to similar projects or evaluating typical changes and classifying whether they are likely to occur on this project. Even if changes are not included in an updated scope at the start of the project, they could be listed in the risk register and managed with greater confidence there.

Managing resources seems to be the largest issue in projects, based on the avalanche of courses offered to project managers on how to manage people. Project managers are high value targets for improving communication and managing people. Therefore, it must be tricky. I always liked two characters that helped me learn how to manage people and communications. The first was the columnist "Dear Abby," which most people have forgotten. Dear Abby was a help column where people submitted their problems and "Abby" replied with well-grounded, sensible advice. Here is my version of an email for project managers.

Sample: Dear Paul
My parents are getting divorced, and my best friend says I'm ugly. My brother was arrested last week for stealing a car. I think the dog does not like me anymore, because he no longer sits with me at breakfast when I eat my chocolate bar and drink a Pepsi. Should I get a new dog? By the way, I am supposed to complete my project task this week, and the instructions are confusing, so that's not going to happen.

Dealing with people can require the diagnostic skill of a doctor and the communication skill of an angel. Regardless, the column was fascinating to read, and I learned to be more upbeat and diplomatic when responding to people's problems. Can AI give us a personality assessment so that the project manager has a better chance at communicating appropriately? I hope so. (See the section on stakeholder management in chapter 3).

The second character I liked is actually not a character but a team. I coached kids' soccer for a few years, mainly for eight- to ten-year-olds, and that is where I honed my listening skills. If parents complained, I tried my best to have them solve their own problems, but when children had a problem, I squatted down to their level and listened carefully. Then I summarized what I thought they said and repeated it back to them while nodding. By then they were normally already much happier, although I would continue to give guidance or help them out. I also learned never to let it go. If they told me about a problem, it was my responsibility to keep track of it until it was obvious that it was no longer an issue. Adults can be less forgiving if you promise something and don't follow up. I don't know if this story can be the basis for a machine learning tool unless it can take conversations and classify them as actionable or simply listen and move on.

Two aspects of quality can be addressed in projects. The first and most common one describes a quality management plan, which addresses how the project ensures the product or service is delivered with the expected level of quality. This can be accomplished with measurements and processes that build the quality into the final deliverable.

The second part is the quality of the project management process, or more specifically, the quality of the methodology being used. If a machine learning tool measures the success factors of projects and then compares them to the methodology used in each project, that might give some insight into how to achieve a higher project success rate. For now, we know that the project methodology must and will change, because it does not deliver a consistent success rate of 95 percent or more for all projects in terms of scope, schedule, and budget.

In larger organizations there will be more than a single concurrent project, and there are likely interdependences with other projects. The projects might be using a common resource, depending on a deliverable or document to be complete at a certain date from another project, or expecting lower costs based on shared purchases of common items. The main dependencies are easy to track, but with all the activity in the exciting project execution stage, many of these interdependent crossovers can be lost. An automated system will be able to maintain a perspective and notify the project manager when there is a risk. However, a machine learning tool might be able to evaluate the entire portfolio of interdependences and make a better prediction of where weaknesses exist that need to be resolved.

PROJECT CONTROL

The project control process is ongoing and is the important collection of metrics in order to identify the project status. It provides important data that can be used as input for machine learning tools. Not only is the raw or current data valuable, but derived data such as trends can also be used. Therefore, it is important to capture the appropriate metrics, make sure the data is consistent and clean, and ensure the data is stored in an accessible repository or a database format that is readable by an AI tool. The basic metrics for status and schedule are always important. However, there will be other input data that a machine learning tool needs, such as quality metrics, risk events, progress and status of contracts, change requests, and changes in the tolerances of stakeholders. Capturing the data is important.

Budget monitoring is a good example of this process. Why is my project over budget? In order to avoid overspending a budget, it is important to ensure accurate estimates at the start of the project and then proactively manage the project budget by evaluating the budget forecast as the project is executed. A machine learning tool that can make better budget predictions will be invaluable. To build confidence into a project budget, a review of historical data can reveal anomalies or variances that may not be evident. Finding a correlation in the data is exactly what a good machine learning algorithm can do. Classification can be used to discover a variety of potential issues with costs. The data can compare a series of successful projects with the current project to identify any concerns or areas that require contingency.

As a professor, I teach a project cost and finance course, so I feel obligated to include earned value management (EVM) as part of using AI in project management. The important cost tracking metrics are cost performance index (CPI), schedule performance index (SPI), and more specifically, monitoring the trends of those metrics and comparing them to other aspects of the project. Machine learning is about correlating data and, in this case, correlating project data. It will be an interesting exercise to assess what correlations are in projects as the CPI and SPI trends show better or worse performance. Can we classify positively trending CPI with data in the project, and can we identify negatively trending CPI with data that could not be uncovered without the help of a machine learning tool? Similarly, with SPI trends from a massive amount of project data, is there a project characteristic that is unique to the trends?

Calculating the estimate at completion (EAC) and variance at completion (VAC) for the project requires simple math. However, a machine learning tool can verify the accuracy of the values. What do you use for estimate to complete (ETC)? Which model is best based on your project data to date? A machine learning algorithm can use historical data to ensure that the ETC and forecast of project costs are more accurate.

The same method can be used to forecast a more accurate project completion date, although it is more complex due to the proper calculation of the critical path and all the possible implications of critical path changes based on task durations being met. Using AI for schedule prediction and classification will likely be one of the most complex tasks. Schedules have a critical path that can shift as the project progresses. There are also a series of dependencies such as resources or other items that have an impact on tasks starting or being completed. Milestones are used to identify when a series of dependent tasks is completed. Perhaps the complexity of the data is ideal for a machine learning tool because completing a project on time is a big challenge for a lot of projects. It will take creativity and insight to determine where and how AI tools can be used to eliminate schedule issues.

The objective is to discover why a project is going to be late, but the schedule is simply a reflection of the impact of other factors, such as a resource issue or a risk that took longer to resolve than was planned. The project end date is based on the critical path, so the analysis needs to assess ways to manage the critical path. This is where existing tools use methods such as checklists, simulation, and predictive analytics. The challenge will be figuring out how to overlay machine learning capability to make these tools more effective than they currently are.

Academic researchers use statistics to find correlations or to recommend the "best" project management processes. A machine learning tool finds these correlations without all the work, thus making some of the academic research into project management obsolete.

Instead of using theories and hypotheses, the machine learning tool can uncover the specific correlations that make your project successful by searching the data. These might include a hidden problem that is unique to your organization or your projects that only an AI tool can discover and reveal.

PROJECT CLOSE

The closing process is more important now that organizations are using machine learning tools. In the closing stage, the project manager must ensure that all the project data is captured and stored in an accessible format. Also, the data needs to be labeled where appropriate so that a machine learning tool can either access the data or use it to update an existing algorithm for reinforcement learning.

One example of making sure that datasets are labeled is the project issues report. The actions that resolve the issue should be identified as successful, and actions that did not resolve an issue should be labeled as unsuccessful. A machine learning tool can then use all the data to classify or predict the best action given an issue that arises in a project that has similar circumstances.

The same is true for risks. At the end of the project, the risks and risk mitigation plans need to be identified with sufficient data for a machine learning tool to use. The lessons learned document must be created and the data captured for future projects as well as machine learning tools that can use the data in a number of ways, such as for project planning and for issues resolution in the executing process. All the results must be stored properly as clean data, which makes it easier for all AI tools to access and use. This stage of the project is no longer a low-value administrative closure. It is now an essential data collection point that has dependencies for the AI tools that can provide significant improvements in future projects.

PROJECT TERMINATION

In spite of all our efforts, there are times when a project is stopped before it reaches the end goal. There are times when a project is deliberately shut down and times when it should be stopped based on the project data. For example, a project can be stopped because a board or project steering committee refuses to grant more funding. Typically, this happens when projects continue to miss deadlines and need more money to pay resources because the scope or amount of work was underestimated.

In some cases, the business case or reason for completing the project is no longer valid. One or both sides of the cost-benefit equation have changed dramatically. Either costs have increased or the value has decreased, or both. This can be difficult to assess when you are in the middle of that crazy exciting executing stage, so a machine learning tool with sufficient data can be used to assess this.

An internal issue can be lack of skilled resources as well as other reasons why tasks are taking longer to complete and costing more. External issues include but are not limited to higher-priced materials, contracts, and a decline in access to resources. There may also be international laws or regulations that change and create obstacles to successfully completing the project the way it was originally planned. A decision will be made to either defer the project or shut it down completely. Shutting down a project is a difficult decision, because people do not want to see the finances already spent be wasted. Continuing to fund an exciting project that is destined to fail can be enticing, and this is why a good project prediction tool is valuable.

AGILE IMPLEMENTATION

Will the process strategy determine how well-prepared your organization is to incorporate AI tools for project management? The agile method is based on iterations that produce a result and then make changes to the project as required. This constant feedback loop provides more real-time data and thereby allows an AI algorithm to perform instant analytics and simulation analysis and predict an outcome that may or may not require further intervention in the project management process. On the other hand, the typical waterfall approach has significantly more data in the form of project documents and easily lends itself to the concept of data mining and predictive analytics. Massive amounts of complex data with subtle interconnections can easily be managed by an AI tool that can then define adjustments that need to be made for project success.

If an AI tool can make better decisions in a faster-paced agile environment, it may result in fewer iterations or less change. On the other hand, faster does not always equate with better. Data normally has two major problems when being used for predictive analytics. The first is the problem of outliers. If data is within a normal distribution, small adjustments may be made successfully. If an outlier occurs and skews the data provided to the AI tool, reacting too quickly to such an anomaly could bring disastrous results. The second issue is biased data, and this is a problem for all AI tools. Historical data is not always the greatest predictor of the future. For example, if you want to select the best project manager for a construction project based on historical data, the odds will probably be in favor of a male, because female project managers are underrepresented in this field.

The answer to which project management approach will be able to adapt more easily to AI tools is debatable. It will likely depend on the scope and purpose of the tools developed. The waterfall approach is more naturally prepared to incorporate AI tools that embrace a holistic approach to managing projects. Agile will adapt more readily to tools that target specific issues in the agile processes. Regardless, organizations that understand their data and deliberately prepare for AI will be the first to find value in the impending AI tools that are going to change the way project management is performed.

Any efficiency toward increasing project success rates results in a lean, structured organization. With the predictor tool, a better project selection process can be in place, and the waste or loss of effort from poorly planned projects can be reduced or eliminated. Similarly, other tools being able to access a successful strategy to resolve project issues from a machine learning tool that is trained to find an optimal solution to certain situations exemplifies a lean approach to managing projects in the organization.

Two challenging areas for agile sprints are effort estimation and risk prediction. Machine learning tools can be applied here because they are naturally good predictors based on regression analysis. The issue is to estimate the effort correctly based on the details of previous estimates and results of user stories. Forecasting risks can be accomplished by comparing the current health of the project to historical experience. Some tools used in the waterfall process should also be able to be adapted for agile environments.

CAN AI FIX PROJECT FAILURE?

As project managers we are optimistic. This positive outlook is required in order to start a complex activity like managing a project or managing the exciting phase of project execution where lots of project manager involvement is required. It is difficult to foresee the internal and external influences that create problems and ultimately project failure, such as huge overspending and constantly delayed end dates. There are project schedule software vendors that claim to improve processes using predictive analytics that determine better resource allocation and improved scheduling dynamics. Can this cure project failure, or are they only promoting their own tools? In project management you need to have a good plan and avoid surprises. This is difficult for humans to do. For example, my high school math teacher taught us probability theory. He would say, "You flip a coin three times and it turns up heads each time. What is the probability that it will be heads on the next flip?" The answer is 50 percent, because there are still only two sides to a coin. As humans we are naturally biased by our experiences, whereas machines can easily calculate the probability of a coin flip. Do we really make decisions based on data? Research has suggested that even our memories can be flawed and do not provide a very good recall of events.[18] At least a machine learning tool calculates an outcome based on data. So far, the benefits of a machine learning tool have been expressed in terms of improving the probability of project success. Now let's flip it around and ask if AI can fix all the reasons why projects fail.[19]

Leadership

Leadership is about being confident and making the correct decisions. The easiest way to lead is to win. Check with any sports team that wins a championship, and you will find a team that supports their captain. Winning tends to override any discontent or conflict within a group. The team has the same goal, and achieving that goal is special. The same is true about projects. Imagine delivering a high-profile, complicated, two-year project on time and on budget. There may have been numerous issues along the way, but in the end the pride of accomplishment can outweigh the bad times. The first way AI prevents failure is by providing the project manager with a high probability of winning, not only from the start of the project but also as the project progresses. With AI tools the tasks will be clearly achievable. This is supported by a much better planning stage and project strategy as well as appropriate

---

18 Michael Lewis, *The Undoing Project: A Friendship That Changed Our Minds*, (New York: W.W. Norton, 2016), page 190.

19 R. Discenza and J.B. Forman, "Seven Causes of Project Failure: How To Recognize Them and How To Initiate Project Recovery," paper presented at PMI Global Congress 2007—North America, Atlanta, GA, Project Management Institute, https://www.pmi.org/learning/library/seven-causes-project-failure-initiate-recovery-7195.

risk planning to avoid and mitigate risks along the way. Having a realistic project plan with a high probability of success is a great recipe for success. Using the right tools provides confidence that all the stakeholders will tolerate bumps along the way if they believe the project will be successful.

Communication

The next problem is also related to leadership: communication. Lack of communication, miscommunication, or poor communication is often cited as a reason for project failure. If the project is using a virtual assistant with an intelligent agent, the possibilities of clear and direct communication will be greatly improved. This will certainly be an improvement for remote workers and globally dispersed teams. As discussed in the stakeholder management section of chapter 3, the project manager will have access to recommendations that provide communication based on individual personality, which is significantly more effective. A pulse of the sentiment for stakeholders will also prevent negative attitudes from derailing the project. These are powerful tools, and the capability will be far beyond what we can imagine. The objective will be to adapt them so that they can be specifically used for project management.

The one area that NLP has the most difficulty with is sarcasm. Perhaps some future version of NLP will be able to detect sarcasm based on the speaker and their temperament and will ask for clarification. For now, you can still say with dripping sarcasm, "Oh sure, this project is just great," and NLP will rate your utterance as positive.

Decision-Making

This reason for project failure should be the easiest one to fix. Machine learning tools will be able to optimize every decision in the project even if the decision appears illogical at the time. Because the ultimate objective is to have a successful project, a machine learning tool can be trained to know how a series of decisions can result in a good project outcome. Even for projects that do not finish on time or on budget, a machine learning tool should be able to calculate the best result given the circumstances.

Software can track many projects at the same time and provide a variety of metrics for each project. Analytics can be used to determine which projects are performing well and which ones are doing less well. There are dashboards that give a visual display of status. More importantly, software can track the interdependences among projects and provide early warning of both real and potential problems. You do not want your project to fail because a previous project missed a deadline and cannot provide the input required to complete your project. Machine learning can be used to identify which interdependences are more likely to fail, and perhaps streaming data can be used to predict potential failures in time to make the adjustments necessary to save the project.

Project Sponsor or Client

The project sponsor may have preconceived ideas of the scope that are not clear in the project scope statement. AI tools can use NLP to review and verify that the budget and schedule are obtainable given the scope and whether there are unidentified expectations that need to be revealed as well. An AI tool can review the previous history of projects specific to the sponsor as well as other similar personalities that have a habit of expanding or changing the scope statement. This information can be used by the project manager to clarify the requirements before the project begins.

Also, the sponsor may have threshold levels for various aspects of the project such as budget overspending, schedule delays, risk, or quality. These should be noted before the project begins and do not need AI to calculate them. What AI is capable of is identifying the expected outcomes based on the project variables and hopefully reassuring the sponsor that the probability of achieving the expectations is high.

Politics

There are organizations that do not want a project to succeed for whatever reason. Perhaps a senior member of an organization hopes that a specific project manager will fail and helps that occur. These are project problems that machine learning cannot solve. Having a clear strategy with a successful prediction and risk plan can set the project up for success, but if organizational interference is delivered in a way that causes project failure, an AI tool is unlikely to be able to predict or avoid this.

One of PMI's academic papers outlines the causes for project failure and categorizes them into three groups: people, process, and communication. All of these are easily addressed by AI tools and concepts described previously. The people issues include understanding the technical issues and involving the client or customer earlier and throughout the project in order to manage change. An AI tool can compare historical data to ensure the technical issues are adequately included. Involving the client is always a good suggestion. An AI predictor tool used throughout the project helps keep the project on track, and managing changes is also an important AI capability.

The process issues that promote failure include poorly defined requirements; insufficient validation of project baselines such as the budget, schedule, risk, and quality plan; and a poor implementation strategy. The predictor tool is ideal for indicating the probability of project success based on the strategy. A tool such as ScopeMaster can easily expose poor requirements using NLP and classification techniques.

The final group of failures is the inability to motivate the team and the lack of effort to ensure that they have the skills and tools required to complete the tasks. As mentioned previously, everyone wants to work on a successful project, and with AI tools providing better documents and planning, the team will be more excited to be part of the project. Ensuring team members have the proper qualifications can be performed by a number of IT tools that do not need to have AI, although one with AI will probably be developed. If team members do not have the proper training or skills, something like the predictor tool will detect it and forecast a reduced probability trend.

SUMMARY

The project review in the section above is not intended to provide all the activities and nuances of a project management process. The purpose is to prompt project managers to think about project data and where it comes from. How is data generated, and how can it be used? Once that aspect is understood, the data can be used as input in order to solve the biggest problems in the project management processes. An added benefit is that the same machine learning algorithm can be used for many purposes by supplying it with different input data. Thinking about the large amount of available data at every step of a project and how to use that data is a big challenge when considering a complex process such as project management.

There are a variety of reasons for project failure, and the list could be endless. However, it is time to move away from the idea that any person can fix the project success rate. The goal is to increase project success rates to a consistent 95 percent or higher, and to achieve that, we need to change the project methodology by inserting AI tools into the process.

CHAPTER 5
Acquiring AI Tools

Artificial intelligence is like a gold rush. Every once in a while, someone ends up with fake gold.

EVALUATING AND ACQUIRING AI TOOLS

In their book, *Prediction Machines*, Ajay Agrawal, Joshua Gans, and Avi Goldfarb highlight the economics of machine learning and how it will drive profound economic changes in the world and in our lives. Similar to other resources, as machine learning algorithms and the accompanying infrastructure become less and less costly, the usage will increase. Everything from everyday decision-making to complex strategy development will become more effective due to machine learning, and this will result in an economic improvement.

How can a project manager take advantage of the dramatically lower cost of machine learning tools? AI is a disruptive technology, so the most effective approach is to redesign the processes for managing projects, then find efficiencies within those processes. Improved efficiency will be possible in all areas of project management. Aside from the incremental benefits of efficiency, there will be a need to adopt the most effective tools for a specific organization or type of project. Strategic decisions will be required to determine whether to make improvements in existing processes or completely redefine what the processes should be.

As more AI tools become available for project management, people need to perform thorough research before they decide to procure one. Access to most tools will be easy if they are offered for free with limited features and then as a subscription service for full features, both of which reduce the risk. Three basic concepts should be considered when implementing an AI tool. The first concept is to maximize value, and since AI is a disruptive technology, the greatest value should involve a disruption to the current project management methodology. Simply stated, the tool should change the way you manage projects. Somewhere in your process, the tool will be inserted, and it needs to return significant value compared to the costs. This concept also means that a project manager must ensure that the changes to the way projects are managed are implemented properly.

The next concept is the holistic approach. As project managers, we are responsible for taking an overall perspective of the project, and with each team member concentrating on specific assigned tasks, it is often only the project manager who has the total view of the project. With that in mind, the AI tools implemented should also find a way to consider all aspects of the project. In other words, the tools should not increase quality yet have a side effect of also increasing risk. The tool should not optimize resources if that means reducing quality. These types of tools will deliver lower value, and the project manager may get stuck with explaining and managing the negative and unexpected side effects.

The third concept is ubiquitous project management. This is the ability to manage a project from anywhere at any time. We think of voice commands for this type of tool, but in reality, it means the ability to access project data and make decisions. That includes being able to perform the work from a smartphone or laptop, perhaps with an app that offers the ability to manage the project using logic applied to the project information. Once again, this capability needs to encompass a holistic view. The project manager cannot make good decisions or communicate effectively if there are gaps in the data or negative repercussions that are not taken into consideration.

Why worry about these concepts? In the next few years, a wide variety of AI tools will be developed and promoted to project managers and PMOs. Some will provide value, and some will be useless. There needs to be a good fit for your organization and your type of project. Understanding for how these three concepts function inside an AI tool will hopefully steer the purchasing decisions in the right direction.

I worked for an organization that had large-scale manufacturing software deployed on site that was essential for processing products correctly and within quality limits. After speaking with some of the users, I created a business case for some of the new advanced features and through my persuasiveness received approval to spend over $200,000 on the new software modules. I moved on to another role and a few years later met the IT person who was assigned to implement the new modules. He told me that they had dropped the implementation work because none of the new software features could really deliver the results expected. In addition, implementation was very difficult, and the users had other priorities. I take this lesson with me when considering new software. Many factors are needed in order to be successful when acquiring and implementing new software tools.

As AI tools for project management are developed and become competitive, so will the sales pitches. One vendor sent me a message saying that his software would make all my dreams come true. Now that's funny. I asked about the technical details, such as what training algorithm is used and how to avoid hidden bias in the data, and to this day, I have not received a response. Be forewarned: you see the cosmetic, but you really need to understand how the engine works. Of course, you need both, but it is easier to see the appearance than to make sure that it meets your requirements. The engine is a mystery unless you can unravel it. Perhaps that's where a consultant can be useful. What technology is being used: SVM, random forest, Naive Bayes, or a neural network? What is the expected level of hidden bias? These questions help determine whether this is truly a machine learning tool or whether it is an expert system with lots of rules and responses. If you are lost, you need help from an expert before spending a large sum of money for an AI system.

STRATEGY FOR IMPLEMENTING AI TOOLS

Numerous AI tools for project management are now available, and more are on the way. Which tools should you adopt? Which tools are best for your organization? It is the early stages of AI technology development in general and very early for AI in project management. What can you do to make good decisions with the onset of a proliferation of tools? This section is about strategy. AI is like a rush to find gold. Everyone wants some, and yet how can you make sure that you don't get fooled into acquiring something that is useless? The first step in any strategy is to gain knowledge and become more educated and aware of the technology. Here are some recommended strategies:

- Investigate how the software and data requirements for AI tools fit into your existing IT infrastructure.

- Decide what can provide the greatest value in your project management process. What is the greatest pain: cost overrun, late due dates, resource availability, or another source of trouble?

- Develop a good business case for purchasing and implementing AI tools.

- Recognize the value of project data and set standards for nomenclature and data retention.

- Set clear policies and procedures to oversee the acquisition of AI tools for project management.

- Allow pilot projects to test the effectiveness of AI tools. This is a good way to increase knowledge and discover value at an early stage.

- If your organization is risk averse, follow the industry. Don't lead the adoption of AI tools for project management. Assess what works and then select the best solutions.

- Actively seek collaboration with similar organizations and promote knowledge-sharing opportunities.

- Find a partner who understands how to use AI tools.

- Ensure the project manager has knowledge of how to manage data and how to interpret machine learning results.

One interesting question will be, Which organizations will gain the most from AI, and which organizations will feel pain and subsequently be left behind in the adoption of new technology? The most obvious winner will be larger organizations that have a lot of accessible project data that can be used for data mining to discover anomalies or for machine learning tools to discover patterns of failure or patterns of success. Once these organizations benefit from the value of machine learning tools for project management, they are likely to see a virtuous cycle of improvements. That is, they continue to maintain good data habits, find more interesting ways to improve their project methodology, and accelerate their determination to store structured and accessible project data.

On the other hand, smaller organizations and associations who have very little data to use will suffer the impact of not being able to monetize any value from project data. They will need to find a collaborative approach or simply hope that a preprogrammed machine learning tool from a vendor or contracted company will apply to their projects, something that is not a certainty.

Project managers who accept AI tools and understand the tool limitations and value will be in demand by organizations seeking a competitive edge. They will know what the results produced by AI tools really mean, and they will find ways to use the results to increase project success rates. There will always be stakeholders who fear new technology and refuse to change. Perhaps they believe in the outrageous myth that one day AI will become sentient and take over the world. That fear is unfounded for narrow AI tools such as the ones being developed for project management, so those stakeholders need to find a way to accept the tools and take advantage of what is offered. Project managers and other stakeholders must also be patient, because early adoption of any new technology is never easy. Problems will arise that need to be resolved. Training will be required in order to understand how to use and optimize the new technology. However, the reward is worth it.

One of the benefits of machine learning is that, given enough data, the results will be automatically customized to the specific organization rather than generic, which would provide far less accurate outcomes. Some conditions or circumstances may be similar to those of projects being executed in other organizations, but an organization's culture and processes are usually unique. This uniqueness can be included in the algorithm training process and used to make predictions or classifications that will increase project management success rates.

HOW TO IMPLEMENT AI TOOLS

Here is a suggested step-by-step approach for how to improve your current project processes with AI tools. This is a rather generic description, and you need to select specific tools that will have an impact.

1. Gather metrics regarding the current project success rate. This includes whether projects delivered the original project scope and any and all variances to budget and schedule. It can include any penalties or losses incurred from the project, and these can be used as part of the business case in step 4 below.

2. Document the existing project methodology used by the organization, and please be honest. If there are no clear standards, capture that. Capture the metrics on how projects are tracked

and results are reported. This step is meant to help with understanding how the process will change. There can be both disruptive tools that change the methodology as well as task efficiency tools, as long as the task efficiency tools don't prevent the methodology from changing when disruptive tools are added.

3. Verify that the project data required by the tools is available and accessible.

4. Build the business case for making changes to the project processes. This should be fairly simple if you are improving the project success rate, but quantifying it should be truly inspiring.

5. Start a project that you can use to test the tools and verify the value.

6. Evaluate the results against the business case and the metrics around current success rates.

7. Incorporate the changes into the new project methodology to be used for all projects.

This is only a guideline, and you need to find a way to make it happen in your organization. Every step may be slow, but keep the objective in mind. Our goal is to take project success rates to levels that are awe inspiring. We can do it.

One of the biggest issues to implementation is risk. More specifically, will it make our project management methodology worse and result in a lower success rate? Similar to the Hippocratic oath for doctors, an AI tool should at least do no harm. A deterioration in the process will lead to fear in implementing change—rarely a good strategy. It takes commitment and courage to move forward with an improvement plan, and as long as the knowledge and understanding has been acquired, it has a high probability of improving the process. Some organizations will make a mess of deploying machine learning tools. Can sloppy deployment create bad publicity? Of course. If there is no solid business case and no clear objective or strategy for deploying a particular tool, the chances of increasing the project success rate are low.

Can hackers use AI tools to derail a project? All software tools are vulnerable, although project management tools seem less likely than most to become infiltrated and misused. For a highly visible project, the easiest way to sabotage it is to provide corrupt input data to make the prediction and classification unreliable. The message here is to keep your data safe and protected, something that should be done anyway. Despite the obstacles, there is a clear path to implementing AI tools to improve project success rates. The strategy and steps outlined in this section can help make implementation a lot easier.

Story: Vendor Selection

I was hired as a consultant for a small association that did not have a lot of project management resources. My role was to score the responses to an RFP from suppliers for the deployment of a customer relationship management (CRM) system. An employee of the association scored the financial submissions worth 30 percent of the total score, and I scored the nonfinancial criteria, which was worth the remaining 70 percent. The contracting company that was selected was ranked near the bottom of my listing, so I was surprised to see that they made it to the top three who were granted meetings to convince the organization that they should be selected. It turned out that one solution provider was a low bidder. While they ranked very low on my scoring, they actually won the bid. Can you guess the result? At one of the first meetings, the company's project manager for the software deployment outlined their process and plans. Across the table from me sat a different contractor who had been hired to perform data cleansing on the old system's database. We looked at each other after seeing the project plan and at the same time whispered, "How did these guys win the bid?" They may have quoted the lowest price, but they did not have a successful process methodology. They assigned four different project managers over a year, because the previous ones would quit. They did not take quality or risk seriously among other process issues, which only confirmed their evaluation results on nonfinancial issues. On the financial side, they overspent all estimates and tried various ways to explain it, but the overruns had to be paid for by the association in order to keep the project moving. The moral of the story is that you can have any correlation you want in machine learning, but if the people who make decisions decide to ignore the results, they will likely have to endure the outcomes that were obvious from the beginning. Machine learning can be an incredible tool that increases project success, but there is a path and a process that needs to be followed, and the key decision makers must believe it in and buy into the results.

A ROADMAP

From a PMO perspective, or simply for an organization looking to implement machine learning and NLP, it is no different than other technology in that it needs a roadmap. What is the strategy for implementing AI tools into the project methodology in order to guarantee a success rate of 95 percent or higher? The first step is to define the scope and boundaries, which includes setting a time frame and understanding or creating the vision that will result in AI tools being implemented. The next stage is to assess what tools are a good fit for the project processes based on the desired methodology. This also requires a review of the system requirements, since machine learning algorithms require data. The roadmap will likely include other tools that the organization plans to implement based on system design. The final part is to review and critique the roadmap to ensure it is sound and robust.

The scope review for the roadmap includes an analysis of how the project processes need to be changed or improved, and this might be better data, introducing or increasing agile processes, or more project manager training. There needs to be a clearly identified objective for implementing AI tools. You can perform data mining looking for correlations, but generally you have a strategy before you begin. This applies to machine learning as well. It starts with an objective of what you are trying to accomplish. Then a strategy is created, such as finding and accessing the data, building a machine learning algorithm, training the software, and then predicting or classifying a new dataset. If the outcome does not align with the purpose, you need to start again. In addition, given the newness of and uncertainty over AI for project management, there needs to be a decision around a proof of concept, initial trial, or full-blown implementation.

One of the frequently used tools in project management is a "subject-matter expert." This refers to someone who has experience on many projects and is likely to have more information than a person who is new to the project team. In all cases the new subject-matter expert will be an AI tool. That is exactly what AI brings to project management: a tool that utilizes all available historic information in order to determine the best plans and strategy.

In the IT world, people identify "use cases." These are problems or opportunities to use software to create a solution. What are the problems that need to be solved in managing projects, and how can they be solved using a machine learning algorithm? However, this might result in a piecemeal approach to changing the project management process. The goal should be to disrupt the process in order to consistently achieve significantly higher project success rates.

The second part is to review all AI tools available and decide what to implement. Which tools will provide the most benefit both short term and long term? Although machine learning algorithms are powerful tools, they become even more effective when integrated with other technologies. The Internet of Things (IoT) technology can include sensors capable of informing the project manager when a task is complete. Also, AI has imaging capability that can be used to snapshot a building under construction, for example, and determine what percentage of the work is complete; scan for quality issues or defects; and match both of those to the expected values at this stage of the project.

The predictor tool is a good example of an algorithm that can be integrated into numerous project management software applications, such as scheduling, resource allocation, risk planning, and budgeting. For each of these, a prediction can be made as to the probability of success of the project based on the plan in place or the status of each item as the project is executed.

In this case something in project management such as the requirements traceability matrix might be useful. The machine learning tool understands each requirement and the work necessary to achieve it. As the project progresses and faces resource shortages or budget reductions, the tool can make the appropriate tradeoff on objectives. The highest value objective can be achieved, while the lower value objectives may be deferred or delivered later. AI can place a value on each objective and ensure that they are still valid and achievable as the project makes progress toward the goal.

Of course, it costs money to implement new technology, and most providers now offer a free trial to allow users to get hooked so that using the tool becomes indispensable. This is followed by a subscription-based payment model. The danger, and note that I am biased, is that the organization selects the easiest tools to implement with a good return. This is often called "low-hanging fruit," an expression that I dislike. I have also seen this strategy used frequently in organizations, and it causes two problems. When organizations pick the easy wins, it looks like all changes will be relatively inexpensive. Secondly, it encourages a piecemeal approach to improving a process. Do you really want the greatest gains in project success rates? If so, a comprehensive approach to changing the project methodology is the best plan. If project management is at the heart of your organization's success, it is important to keep the big picture in mind and disrupt the project management processes.

The final step in a roadmap or strategy for AI tools implementation is to keep it current. This applies to both the software tools and the data. After you successfully implement the tools and are getting amazing results, don't forget to have a plan for how to stay current.

In his book, *The 7 Elements of Strategy Execution: Creating a Culture That Will Ensure Strategy Success*, David Barrett provides great insight into defining strategy: Decide where you want to be. Decide where you are now, and then create a plan to get to where you want to go. The toughest part for many people and organizations is truly understanding where you are now. I believe that will be a big challenge for organizations that want to implement AI for project management. Understanding the current state is not only about technical competence and preparedness but also about culture and desire to create and implement a plan for improvements. That plan may include more changes to the current state than you realize.

Can we rely on AI too much? Initial work with AI tools may be encouraging, but it will take experience and perseverance to achieve project success rates that are significantly higher than they are today. In some instances, AI tools will be implemented poorly. In some situations, the data will be insufficient or contain corrupt values, which in turn will lead to incorrect results and predictions. Another problem is that expertise is limited in how AI can and should be applied to project management. It will also take a mindset change. Organizations need a champion to promote the potential of AI tools, and they also need a clever project manager who can work with data scientists to discover an ideal time and place to start and then show the improved results.

SUMMARY

The selection and implementation of AI tools requires a structured approach that is based on a vision of how the new tools will increase project success rates. The strategy begins with understanding the existing project process and formulating a plan to make changes. There is no magic behind the way that machine learning tools work. They use mathematical equations to build models based on data. The cost of developing and implementing AI tools is constantly decreasing, which will result in a greater variety of tools for project management. The selection of AI tools needs to consider a number of factors such as the benefit to the organization and the ability to radically change the existing project methodology.

CHAPTER 6

The Future of AI Tools for Project Management

"Machines can do anything humans can."
—Geoffrey Hinton

THE PROJECT MANAGER AND THE PROJECT TEAM

Projects are used to instigate change in society, and it is a project manager's responsibility to implement these changes successfully. With AI technology, it is now the project manager who is targeted for change. The role of a project manager is going to be different, and the way we deliver projects will change. Yet preparation for AI technology in our function is difficult, because we have no insight into what the changes will be and what we have to do in order to adapt. Instead of being the drivers of change in the environment, we will now be the targets. Are project managers ready for this change?

Change management covers aspects of communication, training, and process redesign. These are the items that need to be addressed for project managers faced with adopting AI technology. Communication is used to alleviate fears and provide an explanation of changes. Training is required in order to ensure that the new technology is used properly. Process redesign happens in order to implement a new way to perform project management. While many of us drive successful change management for our own projects, it is possible that none of this will happen for the change that is going to overwhelm us as project managers.

When people discuss the role of a project manager with regard to changes due to AI, I try to think of it in time phases. In the short term, the project manager needs to be the person who understands the new technology, finds value, and implements it properly. This can only be accomplished by using incredible change management skills. The big issue with changes due to AI is that the new technology changes the project management processes and the way project managers perform their work.

In the medium term, adopting AI requires a project manager to understand the interaction between data and the tools being used to support good project management decisions. In fact, the project manager needs to collaborate with the machine learning tools. This will be the biggest challenge, and many will fail. Some project managers have a difficult time relating to people, so how will they relate to a machine? How will they react to receiving instructions and direction from a software program? Perhaps it will be an improvement for some of them, because it aligns with their insatiable determination to succeed. Some projects will be more about managing accurate and consistent data flows than actually making decisions to manage a project. This will be the longest era in this transition to AI tools for project management. Eventually, as AI tools have more data, are more easily trained, and adapt to the organizational environment, it will become easier for the project manager to work cohesively with AI technology as part of the project methodology. With success, the project manager may be able to manage many more projects at the same time. However, for those project managers who already feel overloaded, it is probably not wise to ask for more work.

The final stage will be an echo of Geoffrey Hinton's belief that AI will be able to do anything that a human can do.[20] At some point in the future, AI technology will be able to make all the same project management decisions as a project manager. In that situation the project manager will be elevated to a PMO level where the project manager oversees numerous projects at the same time. For some people this is unfathomable, and when articles are published with content similar to this, they cough up all sorts of reasons why a machine could never replace a project manager. This is an indication that there will be resistance to change. As project managers we cannot fight technology, so we have to make it work. It will be a long duration with failures along the way, and those failures will be pointed at by the doubters as proof of the inadequacy of machines and the supremacy of a project

---

20 Tony Peng, "Google I/O 2019: Geoffrey Hinton Says Machines Can Do Anything Humans Can," Synched, May, 2019, https://medium.com/syncedreview/google-i-o-2019-geoffrey-hinton-says-machines-can-do-anything-humans-can-460dff834ae2.

manager. Time will tell. However, the urgency to replace project managers will be driven by continued project failure rates.

AI tools can detect correlations beyond human capability. They will perform faster and be able to analyze far more variables than a project manager. This will become essential, especially with large and complex projects. Sponsors and customers will demand higher project success rates that can only be achieved by using AI technology. In a recent study of diagnosing tumors from brain scans, doctors were accurate in 66 percent of the cases, and an AI program was accurate 83 percent of the time.[21] This is not surprising considering the advanced capability of image recognition in AI software. However, the success rate can be increased further if the two work together, and this is a lesson for project managers. Working together with AI can increase project success.

The objective for project team members is to complete their assigned tasks on the project. Although this is an individual responsibility, there are times when collaboration and communication are essential. Will AI change this? A better question is, How will this change when AI tools are implemented? On one hand, AI should be able to improve communication and bring clarity to tasks so that they may be accomplished with greater certainty and possibly with greater efficiency. On the other hand, there are current AI tools that suggest removing team members from a task if they are not performing well enough. Replacing individuals on tasks can be a sensitive issue for project teams and not well received, especially if the AI tools give no consideration to the human elements and reasons for the performance. We would all love to have high-performing team members in every project and on every task, but that is not feasible. Sometimes the assignments must consider

---

21   Yamei, "Chinese AI Beats Human Doctors in Diagnosing Brain Tumours," AI Business, June 30 day, 2018, https://aibusiness.com/chinese-ai-diagnosis-brain-tumours/.

the best fit for employees and tasks. That may not optimize each task, although it can optimize the project work as a whole.

Do the project team members have a role in implementing AI tools? Project team members can be a great source for finding data that can be used for input to a machine learning tool. They also need to be motivated and accept the changes in the project methodology for using AI tools. This will be important, since the implementation of AI tools into project management processes will be similar to most new technology and may not perform perfectly from the start. Those who stick with it will see the rewards. Project team members who understand and work well with new technology will be rewarded for their increased knowledge and ability to adapt to the new reality of project processes.

The most intriguing question is whether the project team can be led by AI tools instead of a project manager. A globally dispersed project team with employees working remotely may not notice the absence of a project manager. In other situations, the team members may not require interactions with the project manager to complete the assigned tasks. Exceptions such as requesting vacation time or a leave of absence are often handled within self-directed project teams in today's work force. Certainly, a lot of less critical issues can be resolved with team interaction and not with the intervention by a project manager. Some people, such as myself, will gladly accept AI tools if it means spending less time in meetings. It should be a standard practice to communicate project issues as soon as they occur to allow immediate communication to the proper stakeholders and to promote faster resolution. This will be important with an AI tool-based process also, but it raises the question of the project manager's role in projects and which parts of those activities are better performed by AI tools.

How will AI influence the value of being certified as a project manager or project team member? Although certification does give a greater sense that the project member has more knowledge than someone who does not have the certification, it is unlikely to change. The value to be considered with regard to using AI for project management will be knowing more about AI technology and understanding how it works. You don't have to be able to write algorithms, but you should know that data is important and which datasets are being fed into the tools. One of the drawbacks of a neural network is that it does not reveal exactly how it arrives at a prediction or classification. A neural network handles more data than a human brain can comprehend, and the correlations are based on adjustments to weights and biases in the model. It is not possible to truly find out how each piece of data has influenced the model. This lack of clear traceability can be a problem for certain organizations such as banks or firms that deal with security issues. At some point someone will find a way to gain insight, because as we know, technology is changing, and AI tools are advancing at a rapid pace. In fact, there will probably be new developments before you finish reading this book.

IS AI INTELLIGENT?

A common theme regarding AI is fear. Sometimes it is simply fear of change, and those people who fear it always will. Other times, it is fear of the unknown and falling for what I call the Hollywood myth of AI. This is perpetuated in movies that have AI becoming self-aware and requiring some extreme act of heroism to save humanity. Undoubtedly, it makes for a great story. In reality, AI is a software program based on mathematical equations. There is a danger, but it is not the Hollywood version. Equations cannot become self-aware. We can make AI look human, talk like a human, and act human, but that is still all based on programmed software. Do you remember dolls and stuffed toy bears where you pulled a string or pushed their belly and they would talk? They would say, "I'm hungry," or, "I love you." Were those toys alive? Of course not. Now we are even better at making inanimate objects appear human by using software programs, and this is creating confusion. In reality, AI is no more alive than those dolls. Below is part of my code for an AI algorithm.

```
class NeuralNetwork():
    def __init__(self):
        self.synaptic_weights = 2 * random.random((4, 1)) - 1
    def __sigmoid(self, x):
        return 1 / (1 + exp(-x))
    def __sigmoid_derivative(self, x):
        return x * (1 - x)
    def train(self, training_set_inputs, training_set_outputs, number_of_training_iterations):
        for iteration in xrange(number_of_training_iterations):
            output = self.project(training_set_inputs)
            error = training_set_outputs - output
            adjustment = dot(training_set_inputs.T, error
            self.__sigmoid_derivative(output))
            self.synaptic_weights += adjustment
    def project(self, inputs):
        return self.__sigmoid(dot(inputs, self.synaptic_weights))
if __name__ == "__main__":
    neural_network = NeuralNetwork()
    training_set_inputs = array([[0, 0, 1,0], [1, 1, 1,0], [1, 0, 1,1], [0, 1, 1,0]])
    training_set_outputs = array([[0, 1, 1, 0]]).T
    neural_network.train(training_set_inputs, training_set_outputs, 10000)
    print "Considering new situation [1, 0, 0,0] -> ?: "
    print neural_network.project(array([1, 0, 0,0]))
```

This is a simple neural network that analyzes data and predicts an outcome. This outcome is the basis for making decisions at various stages in a project. The real danger of AI is with the creators of the algorithms. Software programs can be powerful enough to cause significant problems for people. Imagine a program used to maximize a crop of soybeans that gets out of control and expands to where it is destroying other crops. That is a real danger, but it does not mean the software is self-aware. It is time to put aside fear and decide how to take advantage of AI technology as well as how to manage and control the creation of programs that might have a detrimental impact on our world.

Despite evidence to the contrary, many fearful prophets still claim that AI will somehow become sentient and take over the world. We know that AI consists of equations based on statistics and calculus to make decisions, and these equations are coded in software. Forget these facts, because Hollywood has a more exciting version where AI becomes self-aware and either wants human rights or wants to take over the world and kill humans in the process. Maybe both will occur, but not in the same movie. Here are some reasons why the Hollywood version of AI is unlikely to become reality:

1. AI software deployment so far is about implementation of practical and narrow-focused decision-making software. A string of equations is at the heart of machine learning, one of the main components of AI. Can $x + y = 1$ suddenly become alive? If so, will it not look at itself and think, "Hey, I'm just a stupid equation; how did this happen?"

2. In most scenarios it takes software intelligence a long period of time to build up to the moment of singularity. The problem with this is obsolescence. In other words, if we are currently creating AI programs in R and Python, in several years won't that be like Fortran and COBOL, two very old and outdated software tools? They are likely to break without maintenance or simply stop working because they are unable to interface with newer systems.

3. There is a famous phrase, "Follow the money." It is this mantra that led to the downfall of former United States president Nixon and many others. A number of people associated with organized crime are in jail not due to acts of violence but because of tax evasion. For an AI to become self-aware and take over the world, it will need to acquire more capacity in terms of server hardware, storage, and network bandwidth. Who is going to pay for this? The AI doesn't have a job or a business with a steady source of income. It cannot suddenly turn to money laundering or fraud.

The human brain is estimated to contain around 800 billion neurons, and scientists suggest that it may be possible for the brain to grow more. The brain also contains around 150 trillion synapses.[22] Researchers are constantly creating larger AI neural networks, and for a neural network to be close to that level, it will take a significant amount of computer memory and processing power.

4. Another problem is that there is no single collaborative effort to complete artificial general intelligence, which means there will be different versions with conflicting objectives. This reduces the amount of total resources available to create and implement each version and, therefore, reduces the probability that any of them will achieve singularity. If the AI algorithms become alive in this scenario, they will probably have to fight each other, which would make yet another interesting movie.

5. Why does AI have to be malicious? It is much more probable that machine learning software code includes morals and ethics than how to be a bad guy and find devious ways to kill humans.

It is possible that some AI algorithms will become aggressive with their objectives and lead to bad results. An example of this would be

---

22 Helen Shen, "Does the Adult Brain Really Grow New Neurons?," Scientific American, March 7, 2018, https://www.scientificamerican.com/article/does-the-adult-brain-really-grow-new-neurons/.

a program designed to optimize potato production that inadvertently wipes out other crops. With narrow AI this is possible, but there is always a plug that can be pulled to stop the program, just like the interrupt key sequence on your computer.

One real danger is that a super intelligent learning program gets out of control and does not have a clear objective. If that happens, we have to believe that organizations are protecting their networks and data in a secure way so that any runaway program is unable to initiate any problems that adversely affect the human population. If a super intelligent AI is created, why does it have to be evil and do bad things that result in the end of humans? Instead, it might find a way to end famines, reverse climate change, and increase the standard of living for everyone around the world. AI might be able to improve the way we interact and communicate with each other, leading to a more positive world order. And it might find a balance between the environment and consumption that stops the extinction of animal species, including ourselves. I am an optimistic person. I believe that we have enough experience with advanced technology that we know how to direct the results toward positive outcomes and not let software programs create havoc.

AI AND ETHICS

When talking about ethics, many people have their own misconception of AI. They ask about AI making serious errors or doing something that causes harm. These are valid questions, but they are asked with an assumption that AI is self-aware. They need to get past the Hollywood myth of AI. We need to set a high standard of ethics for technology companies, especially ones that are creating and using AI tools. The ethics of AI-based decision-making will be based on several factors, including the following:

Data access. AI programs are based on access and analysis of historical data. If your organization and past projects include questionable ethical decisions, that is how the AI will be trained. The technology tools will mimic your organizational culture and bad habits. What are you doing to ensure that your projects meet and exceed high ethical standards?

The programmer or organization that creates the tools. When Microsoft creates a program like MS Word, and it has a bug, Microsoft is responsible. It issues an update to resolve the flaw. With social media tools such as Facebook and Twitter, there is increasing global pressure to manage content so that it meets ethical standards. For ethics in AI tools, the same principle applies. The creator of the technology is responsible for the process that allows an AI tool to make decisions. How are AI tool creators going to ensure that ethical standards are included in the products they produce? There are currently no regulations, although this may eventually change.

Will AI be invasive? This depends on how organizations implement it. Some businesses store user data so user habits can be analyzed and users can subsequently be targeted for individual marketing. Aggressive organizations acquire user data for marketing purposes by sending out web crawlers that not only perform data mining but also hide in places such as routers and capture every personal click in order to build a profile. Other businesses take user data and train the machine learning algorithm without the need to store user data. For project management, the project team and project stakeholders are the ones who are most vulnerable to privacy concerns. Current tools assess how efficient team members are at completing a task and then may recommend a replacement based on habitually slower work. Is that fair? What is affecting the individual's work habit? Is this week an aberration in their normal energy level? An analytics tool can calculate the level of inefficiency of an individual that can be used to determine if they should be replaced.

Monitoring communication and the security of data are two important issues. As reviewed in the stakeholder management section, a tool can help manage stakeholders more effectively with personal data. Problems occur if the data is misused or stolen. These issues need to be properly addressed in order to overcome resistance to the implementation of AI tools.

THE RAPID ADVANCE OF AI TOOLS

The mathematics behind software programs that use machine learning have been around for many years. In fact, neural networks are now a commodity. An internet search turns up numerous programmers who offer free sample code for simple neural networks, and often these are sufficient for the creation of project management tools. Websites such as GitHub have code repositories, and Stack Overflow offers an inspiring comradery of help toward making software code work. There is an unprecedented level of cooperation. In the gig economy, sites like Fiverr offer contracted services to create programs as long as you have funds and a sufficiently well-developed scope statement.

There are other ways to perform machine learning for classification and prediction, such as support vector machines, random forest, Naive Bayes, k-nearest neighbor, and even logistic regression. However, one of the most noted developers of neural networks, Geoffrey Hinton, believes that deep learning with neural networks is the most effective and outperforms any other method. In fact, in creating the predictor tool, the researchers tested other methods and found that the neural network was indeed the most accurate. Neural networks are becoming common, which means that they will be less expensive and easier to acquire.

If neural networks are easy to obtain and use, and they are undergoing constant improvements, then project management tools will only be limited by our imaginations. If we can think of a tool that can be useful, then it can be created and implemented cheaper and faster than any previous technology. The first challenge is to allow our creative side to apply the concept of machine learning to any problem and find a solution that improves project outcomes. The second challenge is to avoid being swamped by the onslaught of AI tools for project management that are like a giant wave heading toward us. We need to select the tool or tools that provide the greatest value. That might be a generic tool, or it might be one that specifically works for one type of organization or project. As project managers, we create business cases for projects that provide value to the organization. Now we must do the same in selecting the AI tools that we want to adopt.

SUMMARY

Project managers have a critical role in the adoption of AI tools for project management. They will be responsible for the appropriate collection and use of data, as well as the successful integration of AI tools in the new project methodology. Project managers need to be champions of the true picture of this technology while, at the same time, their activities become the target of change. Ethics and personal privacy are two important factors that need to be carefully managed by organizations because the implementation of AI tools for project management will bring new challenges in these areas. Advances in AI technology and the availability of numerous new AI tools for project management will test our ability to find and implement the right solutions.

CHAPTER 7
Conclusion

People are not responsible for project failure. It is the project methodology that needs to change.

CONCLUSION

I started this book by challenging the effectiveness of our existing project management processes. Yes, this is a call to action for everyone involved in project management. Ignore the criticism of AI and embrace machine learning tools, because that is the only way project success rates will increase to a level representative of the professionalism to which this career aspires. It is time to disrupt project management by finding ways to insert machine learning tools into the project methodology.

The current project processes are inadequate for obtaining the project success rates that we deserve. AI tools offer the greatest opportunity to improve project outcomes. People are not deliberately causing project delays and cost overruns. Project problems are symptoms of a poor project process and indicate that the tools needed to change the process are missing. Cost is not really a concern based on the way tools are priced, because the value to the project is easily returned. Our will and determination will be the obstacles. Do we really want to change, or do we want to continue the embarrassment of failure? It may be a tough road, so get ready and do your best.

How can we accelerate the introduction of AI into the process? The first step is to ensure that project data in the organization is structured and accessible. We also need to be alert to vendors and anyone who claims that automated tools can perform as effectively as machine learning algorithms. The process needs to be disrupted, not adjusted. Of course, this means that the role of the project manager will change. Project managers need to be the leaders of change. There is a definite career risk in promoting change by implementing AI tools in project management, because it is a new technology, and there is no guarantee that it will perform flawlessly. It will take time, effort, and increased knowledge by project managers and team members to be successful, and these are the exact attributes that will make them more valuable in the inevitable upcoming wave of change in project methodology.

There will be obstacles as well as moral issues to resolve, and they are unpredictable before the process begins. The method to instigate change needs to follow a series of steps typical of initiating a new project, except this time the project is to dramatically change the way that project management works. AI will surpass all expectations once it is integrated into the new project methodology. We deserve projects that deliver the project scope on time and under budget for every project. It is time to make this a reality.

References

A Guide to the Project Management Body of Knowledge (PMBOK Guide), 6th ed., (Newton Square, Project Management Institute Inc., 2017).

Ajay Agrawal, Joshua Gans, and Avi Goldfarb, *Prediction Machines: The Simple Economics of Artificial Intelligence*, (Boston: Harvard Business Review Press, 2018).

Chris Albon, *Machine Learning with Python Cookbook: Practical Solutions from Preprocessing to Deep Learning*, (Sebastopol: O'Reilly Media, 2018).

Hanae Armitage, "X-ray Results Can Provide Higher Accuracy than a Trained Technician," Medical Xpress, November, 2018, https://medicalxpress.com/news/2018-11-ai-outperformed-radiologists-screening-x-rays.html.

Benjamin Bengfort, Rebecca Bilbro, and Tony Ojeda, *Applied Text Analysis with Python: Enabling Language-Aware Products with Machine Learning*, (Sebastopol: O'Reilly Media, 2018).

Nick Bostrom, *Superintelligence: Paths, Dangers, Strategies*, (New York: Oxford University Press, 2016).

Brian Christian and Tom Griffiths, *Algorithms to Live By: The Computer Science of Human Decisions*, (Toronto: Allen Lane, 2016).

Hoa Khanh Dam, "Towards Effective AI-Powered Project Management," Proceedings of International Conference on Software Engineering, Dec 27, 2018, https://arxiv.org/abs/1812.10578.

Paul R. Daugherty and H. James Wilson, *Human + Machine: Reimagining Work in the Age of AI*, (Boston: Harvard Business Review Press, 2018).

R. Discenza and J.B. Forman, "Seven Causes of Project Failure: How To Recognize Them and How To Initiate Project Recovery," paper presented at PMI Global Congress 2007—North America, Atlanta, GA, Project Management Institute, https://www.pmi.org/learning/library/seven-causes-project-failure-initiate-recovery-7195.

Pedro Domingos, *The Master Algorithm: How the Quest for the Ultimate Learning Machine Will Remake Our World*, (New York: Basic Books, 2018).

Ellen Friedman, "Practical Tips for Data Access and Machine Learning Tools," Mapr, April 9, 2018, https://mapr.com/blog/practical-tips-for-data-access-and-machine-learning-tools/.

Ellen Friedman, "AI, All Over the Place: Where Does Artificial Intelligence Pay Off?" Mapr, October 23, 2018, https://mapr.com/blog/ai-all-over-the-place-where-does-artificial-intelligence-pay-off/.

Aurélien Géron, *Hands-On Machine Learning with Scikit-Learn and TensorFlow: Concepts, Tools, and Techniques to Build Intelligent Systems*, (Sebastopol: O'Reilly Media, 2017).

Colin Hammond, "Analyzing the Text of User Stories", www.scopemaster.com, (accessed August 15, 2019).

Arne Holst, "Artificial Intelligence (AI) Funding Worldwide Cumulative Through March 2019, By Category," Statista, May 8, 2019, https://www.statista.com/statistics/943136/ai-funding-worldwide-by-category/.

Marc Lahmann, Peter Keiser, and Adrian Stierli, "AI Will Transform Project Management. Are You Ready?" PwC Switzerland, September 7, 2018, https://www.pwc.ch/en/insights/risk/transformation-assurance-ai-will-transform-project-management-are-you-ready.html.

Kai-Fu Lee, *AI Superpowers: China, Silicon Valley, and the New World Order*, (Boston: Houghton Mifflin Harcourt, 2018).

Michael Lewis, *The Undoing Project: A Friendship That Changed Our Minds*, (New York: W.W. Norton, 2016).

Jeff Loucks et al., "Future in the Balance? How Countries Are Pursuing an AI Advantage," Deloitte, May 1, 2019, https://www2.deloitte.com/insights/us/en/focus/cognitive-technologies/ai-investment-by-country.html.

Mona Mitchell, David Barrett, *The 7 Elements of Strategy Execution: Creating a Culture That Will Ensure Strategy Success*, (Scotts Valley: CreateSpace, 2018).

Cathy O'Neil, *Weapons of Math Destruction: How Big Data Increases Inequality and Threatens Democracy*, (New York: Broadway Books, 2016).

Orny Adams (website), www.ornyadams.com.

Dave Philipps, "The Military Wants Better Tests for PTSD. Speech Analysis Could Be the Answer," *The New York Times Magazine*, April 19, 2019, https://www.nytimes.com/2019/04/22/magazine/veterans-ptsd-speech-analysis.html.

Gil Press, "Cleaning Big Data: Most Time-Consuming, Least Enjoyable Data Science Task, Survey Says," *Forbes*, March 23, 2016, https://www.forbes.com/sites/gilpress/2016/03/23/data-preparation-most-time-consuming-least-enjoyable-data-science-task-survey-says/#11ec00896f63.

Sarah Rieger, "At Least Two Malls Are Using Facial Recognition Technology to Track Shoppers' Ages and Genders Without Telling," CBC News, July 26, 2018, https://www.cbc.ca/news/canada/calgary/calgary-malls-1.4760964.

Helen Shen, "Does the Adult Brain Really Grow New Neurons?," Scientific American, March 7, 2018, https://www.scientificamerican.com/article/does-the-adult-brain-really-grow-new-neurons/.

Raj Singh, *Artificial Intelligence in Banking and Finance: How AI Is Impacting the Dynamics of Financial Services*, (New Delhi: Adhyyan Books, 2019).

Raj Sumit, *Building Chatbots with Python: Using Natural Language Processing and Machine Learning*, (New York: Apress, 2018).

Alan Turing, "Computer Machinery and Intelligence," Mind, Volume LIX, Issue 236, October, 1950, pages 433-460.

University of Vermont "AI can detect depression in a child's speech." ScienceDaily. www.sciencedaily.com/releases/2019/05/190506150126.htm (accessed September 8, 2019), https://www.sciencedaily.com/releases/2019/05/190506150126.htm.

C. Vandersluis, "Panning for Gold by Data-Mining Your Project Tracking Data," paper presented at PMI Global Congress 2013—North America, New Orleans, Project Management Institute, https://www.pmi.org/learning/library/project-data-mining-techniques-5854.

Yamei, "Chinese AI Beats Human Doctors in Diagnosing Brain Tumours," AI Business, June 30 day, 2018, https://aibusiness.com/chinese-ai-diagnosis-brain-tumours/.

Lectures and Talks

Plamendon Angelov, "Autonomous Learning for Autonomous Systems," Machine Learning and Artificial Intelligence Ottawa, Sept 2018.

Keyfer Mathewson, "Shopify, ML and AI in the Browser," Machine Learning and Artificial Intelligence Ottawa, March 2019.

Tony Peng, "Google I/O 2019: Geoffrey Hinton Says Machines Can Do Anything Humans Can," Synched, May, 2019, https://medium.com/syncedreview/google-i-o-2019-geoffrey-hinton-says-machines-can-do-anything-humans-can-460dff834ae2.

Stephen Thomas, "AI and Analytics in Business," Machine Learning and Artificial Intelligence Ottawa, May 2018.

Acknowledgments

I initially planned to research and publish an academic paper on AI being applied to project management. However, I did not find any significant research or theories that I could build on or enhance. The models in this book are mine in conjunction with the fabulous people that I work with in the project management program at Algonquin College in Ottawa, Canada.

A big thank-you goes to the college, especially Jacques, who hired me many years ago to teach my first course in project management. A big thanks also to all my colleagues, who provide support, encouragement, and incredible ideas to our project management program. Your dedication to instilling project management knowledge in so many students is amazing. Thanks to Angela, Nicole, Carlos, Chen, Christine, and Dana. Thanks to Lathif and my other beta readers, Lorraine and Kelly, for clarifying my ideas and giving me direction. Thanks to my wife, Jill, who encouraged me from the start and helped me get through the process with meticulous proofreading and cogent suggestions, and for being such an amazing sounding board. Thank you to the local PMI chapters who invite me to speak and the attendees who cheer, applaud, and ask great questions. I hope to see everyone again with even more practical help on how to incorporate AI into your projects.

Finally, thanks to my students for allowing me to be creative in the classroom.

About the Author

Paul Boudreau, a highly respected and influential project management professional with over thirty-five years in the technology industry, uses his vast knowledge and skills to research and develop AI concepts for project management. His AI prototype prediction tool was recently demonstrated at a PMI-sponsored academic showcase.

As a professor and motivational leader in the classroom, Boudreau has taught more than seventy-five college classes and his public online courses have been taken by students in over 110 countries. His extensive project management experience includes three successful ERP-software implementations within Canada, the United States, and the United Kingdom and has led to collaboration with project management professionals in several countries.

Born in Kingston, Ontario, Canada, Boudreau lives in Ottawa, where he pursues a lifelong ambition to teach and write. He enjoys spending time at his cottage with his life partner, Jill, and their two dogs, Jeannie and Jagger.

Made in United States
Troutdale, OR
12/02/2023